DIVORCE:
God's Will?

The Truth of Divorce and Remarriage in the Bible for Christians

Stephen Gola

DIVORCE:
God's Will?

Stephen Gola

DivorceHope
PO Box 640
301 N. Main St.
Coudersport, PA 16915 USA

Email: info@divorcehope.com
Web Address: http://www.DivorceHope.com
Internet Christian Book Store Web Address:
http://ChristianBookStores.SpreadTheWord.com

Edited by Beverly McKimm
Typeset by Alyssa Dix
Interior Design by Stephen Gola

Front Cover Illustration Given By:
God to Bryan Gola in a dream.

Front Cover Drawn By:
Bryan P. Gola

Cover Design By:
Lori Tomcho Lent,
Ampersand Ink Printing Company

Holy Fire Publishing
531 Constitution Blvd.
Martinsburg, WV 25401
www.ChristianPublish.com

ISBN: 0-9767211-5-5

Printed in the United States of America and the United Kingdom

ABOUT THE BOOK

God uses divorce to save lives! Many divorced people have felt that they have let God down. Those who need to divorce feel that they are going against God's will. But no more! God Himself has spoken on their behalf. The Lord said to the author, "Son sit down, I want to teach you about divorce." DIVORCE: GOD'S WILL? is the result of God's command to help people come out from under the condemnation of religion and to experience His love.

This book is full of hope and compassion! It reveals God's true heart to those who are in a bad marriage and those who have gone through a divorce. There is so much love and power that flows from these pages that it literally releases the reader from condemnation and brings their heart to total peace.

Stephen Gola has never been divorced. He writes the book DIVORCE: GOD'S WILL? purely from the command of the Lord. In early 1992 when the Lord gave him the command to write on divorce, Stephen was a widower though since had remarried.

Since God's Word, the Bible, is the foundation for marriage and divorce, the author has plainly established and made clear from the Bible that God is for divorce and remarriage after a divorce. God cares more for the man and woman who make up the marriage than He cares for the marriage itself.

DIVORCE: GOD'S WILL? covers everything from staying in a bad marriage too long, to that ever-elusive subject, Submission.

TABLE OF CONTENTS

SPECIAL NOTE

The origin of this book did not come by my own intent. I was one among many who were ignorant of what the Bible had to say about divorce. God the Holy Spirit said to me one morning as I stepped from my family room into my kitchen, "Son sit down, I want to teach you about divorce." I immediately acknowledged Him, and gathered up my Bible, concordance and other tools. This book is the result of His command.

I believe many books that have to deal with the tough areas of life have never been written because of the fear of what people will think; fearing that people will misuse or twist the original intent of the book for their own self-gratification, instead of as God intended.

Therefore, I write this book in full confidence as my heavenly Father commissioned me to do. As His Book, the Bible, has been written despite it's misuse, so I write this book. Even as the Bible has been given for our edification, it has become one of the most misused pieces of literature in history. Confidently, God did not hold back on having His Bible written despite His foreknowing its planned misuse. We shall all stand before God one day and give an account of our own actions.

Stephen Gola

INTRODUCTION

A harmonious marriage between a man and a woman is one of the most beautiful and rewarding experiences one can have. But what happens when that beautiful experience is not so beautiful any longer and the love that was so deep has turned into bitterness of heart and hate? What happens when proper counseling has not brought forth the desired fruit, and the hope of the relationship being restored seems lost? And what happens when our spouse turns their back on God, the only true reconciliator of marriages? Is there still hope after all hope appears to be gone? Yes.

As painful as this may sound when dealing with a marriage, divorcing or "making one into two" is necessary and needed to save and preserve life. To save a person's life from the destruction of cancer, a surgical separation must take place. To keep our community safe from a known rapist, they must be separated from the community and incarcerated. A rabid animal must be separated so others may not die also. And as painful as it is, there are husbands and wives who are greatly corrupting their spouse and a separation must take place to save and restore them, before both are lost forever.

This book has been written to save those who make up the family, not necessarily to keep a marriage together. The author recognizes that it is priority to save the marriage, but also knows that some marriages are not meant to be saved, and shouldn't be.

There is a time when the Lord Jesus is our High Priest to bring us together in a marriage; from being two, He makes us one. But there are other times He is our Physician who comes to do surgery as our last resort to bring healing. The surgical procedure of divorce is one of those times. *"...Those who are well have no need of a physician, BUT THOSE WHO ARE SICK. But go and LEARN WHAT THIS MEANS: 'I DESIRE MERCY AND NOT SACRIFICE'..." (Matthew 9:12,13).*

1

GOD'S HEART CONCERNING DIVORCE

CARING TOO MUCH FOR THE WRONG THING

Which is greater in God's eyes: the marriage or the people of the marriage? The priorities in the church concerning marriage have been greatly misplaced. We have judged the "marriage institution" to be greater than the couples who make up the marriage. The institution is NEVER greater than those who make up that institution. A company is only as good as its people. A strong and mighty nation is made up of courageous people who will stand up for what is right under any circumstances. Moreover, a great marriage is great because the couple has a great relationship, and nothing less. **AN INSTITUTION IS ONLY AS GREAT AS THE RELATIONSHIPS THAT MAKE UP THAT INSTITUTION.** When a couple no longer has a great relationship, the marriage is no longer great. When we care more about our marriage than our marriage partner, we have misplaced the emphasis of our relationship. Being married does not create a great relationship. But having a great relationship creates a great marriage.

As Jesus and His disciples were walking through the grain fields on the Sabbath (the day set aside to rest from the weeks activities), *"...His disciples were hungry, and began to pluck heads of grain and to eat. And when the Pharisees [the religious leaders] saw it, they said to Him, 'Look, your disciples are doing WHAT IS NOT LAWFUL to do on the Sabbath!'"* (Matthew 12:1,2). (Also see 1Samuel 21:1-6, 2Samuel 8:17.) Jesus at this point recognized that they had elevated the "Holy Day" that God instituted for man to rest on, higher than the man himself. Jesus immediately responded with an example of violating the Sabbath day and being found guiltless, and also an example of violating the highest institution that exists: the temple where God Himself dwelled, and also being found guiltless.

Jesus said to them, *"Have you not read what [King] David did when he was hungry, he and those who were with him: how he entered the house of God and ate the showbread WHICH WAS NOT LAWFUL FOR HIM TO EAT, nor for those who were with him, but only for the priests? Or have you not read in the law [the Old Testament] that on the Sabbath the priests in the temple PROFANE THE SABBATH, AND ARE BLAMELESS?"* (Matthew

12:3-5). Even though they were guilty of violating the temple of God and the Sabbath day, God Himself did not consider it sin and did not blame them one bit for doing it. They violated the temple of God and the Sabbath day OUT OF NECESSITY, not selfishness or evil.

Jesus continued, *"However, I am saying to you, SOMETHING GREATER THAN THE TEMPLE IS IN THIS PLACE"* (Matthew 12:6 WUEST). And what was greater than the temple? The people and the God of that temple. And what was greater than the Sabbath day? The people for whom that day was made. And who is greater than a marriage? The people who are joined together in that marriage.

When we are faced with the decision of either saving the institution or the people of the institution, the institution must go. And when we are faced with the decision of either saving a marriage or the people of the marriage, the marriage must go. Whether it be the Sabbath day, a company, the ministry, the nation, or a marriage, the people of these institutions are always more important than the institutions themselves. ALWAYS!

Jesus continued, *"And IF YOU HAD ONLY KNOWN WHAT THIS SAYING MEANS, I desire mercy [readiness to help, to spare, to forgive] RATHER THAN sacrifice and SACRIFICED VICTIMS, YOU WOULD NOT HAVE CONDEMNED THE GUILTLESS"* (Matthew 12:7 AMP). God is not looking for a husband, wife or the kids to be sacrificial victims just to "keep the marriage going." He would rather for the marriage to be dissolved and the people of the marriage to go free and not to be condemned.

If we put the institution first, instead of the people, we lose the vision for the institution. The vision of the people makes the institution what it is. Without a vision, failure and collapse are inevitable. When the dreams for the marriage that are in the heart of the husband and wife go out because of a bad relationship, the marriage is on a collision course with a bad situation. But as long as there is vision for the marriage, the marriage will continue. When a married couple loses the vision for the marriage, which is that joy a person possesses in their heart to spend the rest of their days with their mate, it's hard to rekindle on their own. However, God is able through willing hearts.

When the focus is placed on saving the marriage instead of saving the people of the marriage, the process for the marriage to fail starts to accelerate greatly. If the focus is not shifted to saving the couple and making them whole, within a short time, the marriage will completely fall apart. In general, the primary thrust of what is called "marriage counsel" does little for individuals who really need the help. I'm not saying that we don't need marriage counseling, because we do. We just need to change the focus of the counseling from saving the institution of marriage, to saving the couples of marriage. If a person has outbursts of rage, abusive actions or some major vice that's controlling their life, counseling the couple on how to "deal" with each other's problems is like putting a band-aid on a wound with a severed artery. If the life-threatening problem is not directly addressed, the person will die.

In the marriage, the real problems, those old wounds, scars, fears, and pains that manifest themselves as outbursts of rage, abusive actions and controlling vices must be addressed first. If wholeness is not grown in the person, the marriage won't be whole. But when wholeness is developed in the couple first, the marriage will be sound. The best way to save a marriage is to first save the people of the marriage. God is very able and wants to restore broken relationships; but He will not restore a relationship that should be broken.

IS IT THE METHOD, OR THE MOTIVE BEHIND THE METHOD?

Does God hate divorce because of divorce itself, or does He hate the perverted motive that men use behind this method to save?

There is both a right or wrong motive and attitude behind every action. It is no different with divorce. For example, the tenth commandment says, *"You shall not covet..." (Exodus 20:17)*. Is this something that God hates? Sure it is. But is it the things themselves that we covet that are wrong, such as nice

17

clothes, a good car, a decent place to live, healthy food to eat, or is it the motive that says, "I want what you have?"

Proverbs 6:16-19 mentions things the Lord hates, such as:

"a proud look." Is it the "look" that's wrong, or the perverted motive that exalts self behind the look?

"a lying tongue." Is it the "spoken words" that are bad or the heart motive to cover up truth?

"hands that shed innocent blood." Is it the "act of self defense" by killing another person, or the manifestation of hate to murder for selfish motive?

"one who sows discord among brethren." Is it the "sowing of seeds," or is it that the seeds are seeds of division instead of seeds of unity?

Does God hate divorce when it is used to save one or both of the spouses out of a dying marriage so they can get a new start with Him? Or does God hate divorce when the motive comes from a heart that is self-seeking — wanting to push aside the marriage partner He gave them, for "something better." (See Malachi 2:11-16) **THERE IS A DIVORCE THAT GOD APPROVES OF, AND THERE IS A DIVORCE THAT GOD HATES.**

The divorce that God approves of is one of His major surgical procedures to save the people of the marriage (but not necessarily the marriage itself). But it has been turned into something detestable and abhorred. And because of this, many husbands and wives will live life with no joy, dead hearts, and guilt from not divorcing just to save the marriage, but themselves being lost because they were kept from a surgical operation they so desperately needed. Instead of attempting to save the people of the marriage, we want to save the marriage, and forget about the ones who make up the marriage. That's like trying to save a burning building and not caring to rescue the people who work in the building. Do we save the people of the marriage, or do we save the marriage itself for the sake of the marriage? **GOD'S FIRST PRIORITY IS THE INDIVIDUAL, AND *THEN* THE INSTITUTION THESE INDIVIDUAL'S MAKE UP.** If we try

18

to save the marriage, we will probably lose the couple. But if we try to save the couple first, we have a very good chance to save the marriage, but more importantly, we will save one or both of the couple.

When people say, *"God hates divorce"* as quoted from Malachi 2:16, normally that has been taught to mean that divorce is not allowed AT ALL. We shall see that this is only a half-truth.

In Jeremiah the eighth chapter, Jeremiah mourns over the inhabitants of Jerusalem. The Lord gave them a warning through the prophet in verses 4-22. In verse 5, it says that they were *"...in a perpetual backsliding [condition]"* and in verse 9 that *"...they have rejected the Word of the Lord."* Our wrong motives and attitudes will always reject "the Word of the Lord."

Because their motives and attitudes toward God and people were so bad, God said in verse 10, *"Therefore I WILL GIVE THEIR WIVES TO OTHERS, AND THEIR FIELDS TO THOSE WHO WILL INHERIT THEM."* Notice God's attitude concerning the marriage. The marriage itself was not first priority, but second. God did not save the marriage, but broke it up because of their continual disobedience. There is a curse that actually comes upon the marriage relationship because of continual disobedience to God (See Deuteronomy 28:30).

For He said, *"...I will give their wives to OTHERS..." (Jeremiah 8:10a).* "Others" means other marriage partners. Remember: **GOD'S PRIORITY IS TO SAVE THE PEOPLE OF THE MARRIAGE, NOT NECESSARILY THE MARRIAGE ITSELF.** God is the one who broke these marriages up. I believe that the husbands were just as cruel to their wives as they were to the Lord. God didn't even ask the husbands for a Divorce Certificate. He just had another country come and take over. **DIVORCE ITSELF IS NOT WHAT GOD HATES, BUT THE "WHY" AND "HOW COME" BEHIND THE DIVORCE.**

WHEN IS DIVORCE SIN?

Thinking divorce is a sin when it's not can keep us out of God's desire for us to live a life of peace. Many times, we consider something that hurts or causes pain to be "bad," but that is hardly the truth. We all know that there are things that cause hurt and pain, and are bad. These are not our discussion. But let's look at some of the hurts and pains we MUST suffer *"...to LIVE GODLY in Christ Jesus..." (2Timothy 3:12).*

To illustrate this, let's start at the Ten Commandments written in the book of Exodus, the twentieth chapter. The command is *"you shall not murder" (v. 13).* We know to murder someone IS sin. We also know that *"If we confess our sins, He is faithful and just to forgive us our sins and cleanse us from all unrighteousness" (1John 1:9).*

Even though to murder is to kill, to kill is NOT to murder. For instance, God has called out His people many times in the Bible to fight and defend their land so they will not be taken over by another people and lose their freedoms. Because they defended the very soul of their country, they suffered pain. They may have lost lives, but they maintained their freedom. They may have even lost family members who were dear to their heart, but the nation was saved and the children's future was preserved, giving them the freedoms the parents enjoyed. There is pain, there is hurt in being set free from bondage.

If divorce was "always" a sin, then that would mean that God sinned when he commanded the people of Israel to separate themselves from, and divorce their wives they married outside of His will (See Ezra 10:3,11). We know that God does not sin, for He is righteous *"...and in Him is no darkness AT ALL" (See 1John 1:5).* God did not give the Ten Commandments for us to live by while He, Himself, violates them at His will. No, we are assured that when God gives us commandments for direction in life, we know that He keeps them, too. We know that God is true because HE IS TRUTH (See 1John 5:6-7).

IF DIVORCE WERE SIN IN ITSELF, GOD WOULD HAVE NEVER SANCTIONED IT (see 1Corinthians 7:27-28, Deuteronomy 24:1-2). Divorce is not sinful part time and righteous part time.

It is the MOTIVE behind our actions that determine if it is sin or not.

Many times when we hear the word "divorce" we proverbially bow our knees and say, "Oh, another has fallen captive to that 'great sin.'" First off, divorce is not always a sin. Moreover, when it is, it doesn't have "god" status. Meaning, the sin is so great that it cannot be forgiven. Whoever heard of a sin so big that the blood of Jesus Christ was unable to cleanse us from it? For *"...with His own blood He entered the Most Holy Place once for all, HAVING OBTAINED ETERNAL REDEMPTION [FOR US]" (Hebrews 9:12).*

IF THE NON-CHRISTIAN SPOUSE IS WILLING TO LIVE GODLY

"...If any brother has a wife WHO DOES NOT BELIEVE, and she is WILLING TO LIVE WITH HIM, let him not divorce her. And a woman who has a husband WHO DOES NOT BELIEVE, if he is WILLING TO LIVE WITH HER, let her not divorce him" (1Corinthians 7:12,13).

Being "unequally yoked" in any relationship is very unpleasant and can have a significant negative impact upon your life, especially when we are dealing with an intimate union such as a marriage (See 2Corinthians 6:14). Verse twelve and thirteen specifically speak to the non-Christian spouse that is "willing to live" with the Christian spouse. This is where after they were married, one spouse received the Lord as Savior and the other did not, or, the Christian spouse married a non-believer ignorantly or non-ignorantly. In these verses, "willing to live" with someone does not mean to just reside at their residence, but to carry on "a way of life" as God prescribed in the Bible. This "way of life" is a holy life. The next verse (1Corinthians 7:14) reveals clearly the holy life the one spouse is living because they now cause the other spouse and their children to be "sanctified" or, made holy as well.

The rule of 1Corinthians 7:14-16 is: If you have a marriage partner who is willing to not interfere with you serving God with your whole spirit, soul, and body while raising your children in a godly atmosphere at home, allow them to stay. A godly atmosphere will produce godly children. This is God's purpose, for He seeks godly offspring (See Malachi 2:15). You see, even though the non-Christian spouse does not know God in a personal way, and does not hinder you and your children from serving Him, God will bless them just because they yielded to God in your behalf.

However, when a marriage partner is not willing for you or your children to live as the Bible commands and they persist in that manner, you have every godly right to end the marriage, and go free. For *"...IF he is willing to live with her [to give her the liberty to fully live for God], let HER NOT DIVORCE him"* (1Corinthians 7:13). But IF the husband in this case is unwilling to give his wife the liberty to serve God completely, the door and the divorce papers are his portion.

Even though the Bible says, *"Are you loosed from a wife [or husband]? Do not seek a wife [or husband]. But EVEN IF YOU DO MARRY, she [or he] has not sinned..."* (1Corinthians 7:27,28). Beware; every person who has truly become a Christian by accepting Jesus into their heart is not necessarily compatible with each other. I say this strongly because of the importance. Marrying even a Christian who is not compatible can be a disaster. However, through diligent obedience and difficulty, the power of God is available to overcome.

Many times this question arises concerning divorce: "Who is the one who divorces whom? Does the spouse who is doing 'right' divorce the one who is doing wrong? Or does the spouse who is doing 'wrong' divorce the one who is doing right?" It can be either way. It does not depend on the situation as was always believed. In other words, the believed tradition (that "if the **other** marriage partner files for the divorce, then **I** will be free to remarry. But if **I** file for the divorce, I can't remarry") is just that: a made-up tradition that has absolutely no bearing on the situation at all.

Concerning a Christian and a non-Christian marriage, the Scriptures give the right to divorce to the spouse who loves

God. For *...IF any brother has a wife who does not believe, and SHE IS WILLING to live with him, LET HIM NOT DIVORCE her. And a woman who has a husband who does not believe, IF HE IS WILLING to live with her, LET HER NOT DIVORCE him"* (1Corinthians 7:12,13). But if he or she is NOT WILLING, the Christian spouse has the right to divorce their mate. For IF he is willing to let you live for God, don't divorce him. BUT, IF he is NOT willing to let you live for God, divorce him. That is the context. But if HE departs to divorce YOU, let him. You are *"...not under bondage in such cases. But God has called us to peace"* (1Corinthians 7:15).

No marriage partner who truly loves God takes divorce lightly. For even after much abuse, they want to somehow see their spouse delivered from what causes them to act in such a demoralizing manner.

A SANCTIFIED (HOLY) SPOUSE DOING UNHOLY THINGS?

Whether a Christian marriage is equally yoked or unequally yoked, God's command to us is always the same; *"...MAN OF GOD ...PURSUE RIGHTEOUSNESS, GODLINESS, faith, love, patience, gentleness."* As we do this, *"...the unbelieving husband is SANCTIFIED by the wife, and the unbelieving wife is SANCTIFIED by the husband; otherwise, your children would be unclean, but now THEY ARE HOLY"* (1 Timothy 6:11, 1Corinthians 7:14).

To be "sanctified" simply means that there is a process of cleaning up going on in a person's life by God that causes them to be separated from that which is not like Himself and being made into that which is like Himself. (Actually, the words sanctified, separated, holy and hallowed that are used in the Bible are basically the same Greek word. They mean the same thing.) Because the "unbelieving husband is sanctified by the wife," the wife must be sanctified herself and because the "unbelieving wife is sanctified by the husband," would mean the husband must be sanctified himself. And if the "children would

23

be unclean [unholy], but now they are holy," a mother or father MUST be serving God. Between the husband and wife, one being a Christian and the other a non-Christian, someone must give their whole life to God for Him to make the rest of the family holy. I have heard it said all too often that when a husband lives ungodly and the wife wants to live godly, that the wife must stay with her spouse and do whatever he tells her to do no matter what it is because he is the head — even to the point of not serving God. How ridiculous! The wife is seeking for a way out of a bad situation, but is only sentenced back to her prison by "holy men of God." They want to serve God with all their heart, only to find out they must bear the heavy yoke again. Many times this situation ends in tragedy and the so-called "glory" is given to God. Then the spouse who wants to live godly ends up as a "slave of man" instead of a "slave of righteousness."

SLAVES OF MEN OR SLAVES OF RIGHTEOUSNESS?

"But if the unbeliever departs, let him depart; a brother or a sister IS NOT UNDER BONDAGE IN SUCH CASES. But God has called us to peace" (1 Corinthians 7:15).

Notice the word "bondage" in verse 15. The word in the Greek text is *"douloo,"* which is the same word for "slave," or "to be enslaved." Most clearly, when one is in bondage, they are a slave to whomever or whatever has them bound.

Let's read verse 15 from the Wuest translation: *"But assuming that the unbelieving husband departs, let him be departing. A [CHRISTIAN] BROTHER OR [CHRISTIAN] SISTER IS NOT IN THE POSITION OF A SLAVE, NAMELY, BOUND TO THE UNBELIEVING HUSBAND OR UNBELIEVING WIFE IN AN INDISSOLUABLE UNION IN CASES SUCH AS THESE; but God has called us [to live] in peace" (1 Corinthians 7:15 WUEST).*

Notice the "peace" in this case, comes from a separation, not a union. *"...God has called us [to live] in peace" (1 Corinthians 7:15b).* A home that has become a war zone because of two opposing hearts that have been tied together is not peaceful. Being at peace is having the same heart. Again, the Scripture says that a Christian brother or sister "is not in the position of a slave" and goes on to say that they ARE NOT "bound to the unbelieving husband or unbelieving wife in an indissoluble union in cases such as these." Which means, if we stayed in a situation such as this, we would actually become a slave. And if we become a slave, then someone would have to be the master! You can't be a slave without having a master over you. And you can't be in bondage, without someone or something binding you. **THE SLAVE ALWAYS PORTRAYS THE MASTER'S DESIRE.**

If a godly spouse continues to live with an ungodly spouse, the godly spouse will most likely eventually portray ungodliness, which is also reflected by them not growing in God. This is why Jesus bought us with a price, *"...so you DO NOT become slaves of men ...[but] slaves of righteousness" (Romans 6:18, 1 Corinthians 7:23).*

The book of James says, *"Does a spring send forth fresh water and bitter from the same opening? Thus, NO SPRING YIELDS BOTH SALT WATER AND FRESH" (James 3:11,12b).* This is a Bible principle. When sin (salt water), is mixed with holiness (fresh water), that which was holy becomes corrupted and sinful. Thus, no spring yields BOTH salt water and fresh. When polluted water is mixed with clean water, the clean ALWAYS becomes polluted.

The "slave" living under the "master" and the "fresh water" being mixed with the "salt water" is the godly spouse being polluted by the ways and actions of the ungodly spouse. The godly spouse will become a slave and polluted. Good apples in a bushel do not make the rotten apples better. The good become rotten. God is always saying, *"come out of her my people, lest YOU share in her sins, and lest YOU receive of her plagues" (Revelation 18:4).* "DO NOT BE DECEIVED: "EVIL COMPANY CORRUPTS GOOD HABITS. AWAKE TO RIGHTEOUSNESS, AND DO NOT SIN; FOR SOME DO NOT HAVE THE KNOWLEDGE OF GOD" (1 Corinthians 15:33,34).*

STAYING IN A MARRIAGE FOR THE WRONG REASON

"For how do you know, O wife, whether YOU will save your husband? Or how do you know, O husband, whether YOU will save your wife?" (1Corinthians 7:16).

The implication is that we can actually continue to stay married for the wrong reasons. The emphasis here is whether YOU will save your spouse. For when we think we can do God's job to pressure someone to become a Christian or believe the way we believe, we are in grave danger. For NO ONE can come to Jesus *"unless the FATHER ...draws Him..." (John 6:44)*. For we can actually be trying to lead someone to the Lord and be out of God's will because it may not be OUR place or the right time. (However, we are always to be an example of who God is, and what He stands for; not to be slaves, imprisoned by the threats and or beatings of ungodly men.)

The word "save" also means to deliver, heal, restore to proper order, or to make whole. The idea to save is often found in new marriages where one of the partners "thinks" that they can change the other or cause them to be free of some sort of problem such as drugs, rage, alcohol, or crime. But after much pain they find out it doesn't normally work that way. It takes God to change a person's heart and to free them from such things.

The Wuest translation put it this way: For *"ONLY as the Lord has assigned to each one his lot [in life], as God has called each one, IN THAT WAY let him be ordering his manner of life..." (1Corinthians 7:17)*. Many have taken this Scripture to mean that the spouse that wants to walk with God is supposed to submit to the ungodliness of the other spouse. This is foolishness!

The real questions for this Scripture are, "what has the LORD assigned to each of us as our lot in life? As we walk in that assignment, how shall we order our manner of living?" The answer to both of these questions must culminate into this one thing. *"Be holy, for I am holy" (1Peter 1:16)*.

Some have even said that if a wife for instance, is in a bad marriage, whether they're being abused or however their husband is treating them, that that is their lot from God. This is nothing but foolishness and stupidity in its purest sense. They don't know it's the *"...GOODNESS OF GOD [that] leads you to repentance" (Romans 2:4)*. An abusive type of environment in the home is just not good. A healthy home environment is brought about by seeking *"...those things which are above, where Christ is..." (Colossians 3:1)*.

How can a person live a godly life and at the same time submit that life to someone who practices ungodliness? *"For either he will hate the one and love the other, or else he will be loyal to the one and despise the other..." (Matthew 6:24)*. You cannot love the Lord your God with all your heart while lowering and yielding yourself and your children to accept, partake and participate in things that the Lord Himself detests.

What has the Lord assigned as our lot in life? Surely it can't be a life you hate so much you want to die to escape the pain. No! The Scriptures are so powerfully clear. Let's take a look:

For *"...we are the temple of the living God. As God has said: 'I will dwell in them and walk among them. I will be their God, and they shall be my people. Therefore COME OUT FROM AMONG THEM AND BE SEPARATE, says the Lord. Do not touch what is unclean, and I will receive you! I will be a father to you and you shall be my sons and daughters, says the Lord Almighty. THEREFORE, HAVING THESE PROMISES, beloved, let us cleanse ourselves from all filthiness of the flesh and spirit, perfecting holiness in the fear of God" (2Corinthians 6:16b-17:1)*.

If that's not powerful enough, the Scripture also says to, *"Let love be without hypocrisy. ABHOR WHAT IS EVIL. CLING TO WHAT IS GOOD" (Romans 12:9)*.

How could you not hate evil, and truly love, at the same time? That is hypocritical love. Hypocritical love does not hate evil. It allows evil to dwell beside it in its own home. Love MUST hate evil to be true in itself. Let our love be WITHOUT hypocrisy. Otherwise, it's not love at all, but bondage. And for one to "cling" to that which is good, one must at the same time separate from

27

that which is evil. As we move closer to that which is good, there is always a moving away from that which is evil. **TRUE LOVE *ALWAYS HATES EVIL!***

It says in Proverbs 3:6, *"IN ALL your ways acknowledge Him and He shall direct your paths."* How can we, in all our ways acknowledge God and receive direction, if we are united to a spouse who does not want to follow God's ways and doesn't want us to either? The marriage will produce constant strife. God wants us to live in peace.

A LOVE STORY GONE BAD

Let me take you on a journey and we'll follow a man who loved God, but the people he led did not. The man was Moses and those he led were the people of Israel. We will see the struggles and the consequences of caring more about the one we love, rather than the One who first loved us, God.

Even though Moses is depicted here as the leader of his people, he is also viewed as a type of husband to his wife. So Moses is seen as both leader and husband.

It all started when God sent Moses to deliver the people of Israel out from Egyptian bondage. We are talking about four to seven million people. The first things Moses did were mighty signs and miracles in their presence. This outward display of God's ability changed their hearts and affirmed that God truly did love them and came to deliver them. Judgment came upon Egypt because Pharaoh would not let the people go free. God performed many miracles through Moses that caused great devastation on their land and their people (See Exodus 4, 5).

The people of Israel soon learned what it was like to trust God. Miracles seemed to follow them everywhere. God Himself, in the form of a pillar of fire by night and a glorious cloud covering by day, was over their entire settlement and wherever they traveled. He even gave the people of Israel a song of victory as they crossed the Red Sea that we still sing today:

28

"I will sing to the Lord, for He has triumphed gloriously! The horse and its rider He has thrown into the sea" (Exodus 15:1).

However, it didn't take long before the excitement of God's miraculous deliverance wore off and the fear of the unfamiliar raised its ugly head.

Whenever our environment around us starts to change, we naturally start to resist. We are no longer in the familiar. This newness tends to give us a fear about itself. Some of the first words we may speak are, "We've never done it that way before." That's what makes growing up, growing up! We're entering into something or going somewhere that we haven't been before. Haven't we all said, "I wish I would have done that years ago? Look where I would be today." What kept us from doing "that" years ago? Fear! Anyone can do something when it's a sure thing. It requires no faith and no courage to stay in the familiar. If we want to fully mature and grow to our full potential, we must be courageous, and trust God. No matter what befalls us, or what obstacle we encounter, He is able, and He will bring us through.

Three days' travel into the wilderness after crossing the Red Sea, the children of Israel started to complain about needing water (See Exodus 15:22-24). After fifteen days, they considered the journey too hard, they wanted to die. All they could think about was, "how it USED to be, the good times." In fact, most of the "good times" were not good at all. They themselves were slaves. The good times were full of misery. Growing up and learning to trust God is rarely easy, but always necessary. Nevertheless, the complaining continued. Instead of the people of Israel asking God for His provision, they complained to Moses (See Exodus 16:8, 17:2-4).

Despite their habitual complaining, the Lord gave them manna, heavenly bread in the morning and quails in the evening to eat. The Lord sent them water for themselves and their livestock (See Exodus 16,17). This test was to find the people of Israel faithful to God, but instead, they tested God to see if He would follow their demands. This type of response displeased and hurt God deeply.

THE SEPARATING POINT

This is the most critical point of our relationship with God, where we tend to dig our heals in deep and say, "I'm not going any further. I'm comfortable where I am." At this point, if we continually refuse to go on with the Lord into a deeper relationship, we will actually be left to die in the wilderness like the people of Israel. Jesus Himself bore witness of this difficult place where Christians fail. He said, *"...narrow is the gate and DIFFICULT is the way which leads TO LIFE [the third level of spiritual maturity], and there are FEW who find it"* (Matthew 7:14). This is a major point of strife, which can cause a separation in a relationship. One spouse wants to fully serve God and the other spouse resists.

God gave the people of Israel a glimpse of the Promised Land and the difficulties that had to be overcome in obtaining it. And what a great place it was. The twelve spies that were sent out returned to bring back the report:

They *"cut down a branch with one cluster of grapes; [it was so big] they carried it between two of them on a pole"* (Numbers 13:23). And ten of the spies said, *"It truly flows with milk and honey, and this is its fruit. NEVERTHELESS, the people who dwell in the land are strong; the cities are fortified ...[it's] a land that devours its inhabitants... and we were like grasshoppers in our own sight..."(Numbers 13:27b, 32b,33b).*

Now you could see why the Lord said, *"...DIFFICULT is the way which leads to life."* God called the last part of the report that the spies brought back, as evil. **THEY FOCUSED ON THE OBSTACLES THAT WERE IN THEIR WAY INSTEAD OF ON THE ONE WHO PROMISED TO BRING THEM THROUGH.**

The situation looked impossible, and so it was with man's strength. However, God never intends for us to do His will with our own ability. He never intends for us to go through a divorce in our own ability. We will always look like grasshoppers in our "own" sight.

This really created a lot of fear in the people of Israel. Instead of embracing change with courage for betterment, they rejected it because of fear and that generation forever lost out. *"And all the children of Israel complained ...[and] ...said to them, 'IF ONLY WE HAD DIED in the land of Egypt! OR IF ONLY WE HAD DIED in the wilderness! WHY HAD THE LORD brought us to this land to fall by the sword, that our wives and children should become victims? WOULD IT NOT BE BETTER FOR US TO RETURN TO EGYPT?'"* (Numbers 14:2-3). Remember, Egypt means bondage, slavery, much abuse. Because they refused to take courage and face the problem, and to trust God that He knew what He was doing, they by default chose to stay in a bad situation.

This struck the Lord right in the heart. He said to Moses, *"HOW LONG will these people reject me? And HOW LONG will they not believe me, with all the signs which I have performed among them? I will strike them with the pestilence and disinherit them, and I will make of you a nation greater and mightier than they"* (Numbers 14:11-12). God is NOT saying that we will miss out on Him if we leave those behind who are keeping us from doing His will. But our portion and blessing from God will be greater if we DO leave them behind, because He said, *"...I will make OF YOU a nation GREATER AND MIGHTIER than they"* (Numbers 14:12). Who knows how mighty and great a nation Israel would have been today if only that Moses said, "Yes" to God?

There comes a point in time as we continue to rebel when the Lord will stop showing His grace toward us. We can actually know in our heart what God wants, and continue to pray for something else until we frustrate His grace. At that point, God will give us what we want. How sad.

THEY BOTH LOST OUT

"And Moses said to the Lord: 'Then THE EGYPTIANS WILL HEAR IT, for by your might you brought these people up from among them, AND THEY WILL TELL IT to the inhabitants of this land. SAYING, 'BECAUSE THE LORD WAS NOT ABLE TO BRING THIS PEOPLE TO THE [PROMISED] LAND WHICH HE SWORE TO GIVE THEM, THEREFORE HE KILLED THEM IN THE

WILDERNESS.' And now, I pray ... PARDON THE INIQUITY OF THIS PEOPLE ...according to the greatness of your mercy, just as you have forgiven this people, from Egypt even until now" (Numbers 14:13,14a,16,17a,19).

Moses presented what appeared to be a great prayer on their behalf. But it wasn't. God was fed up; He was pushed too far; His favor had ended. No more would they enjoy life because of their rebellion. Even though God told Moses, *"I have pardoned according to your word" (Numbers 14:20).* God didn't forgive them without severe discipline. From then on, God would actually restrain the Israelites from prospering until that first generation had died.

Because of the Israelite's continued unbelief and rejection of the Lord, God was ready to kill them and start all over with Moses to make him a nation greater and mightier than what He had originally planned for them. Obedience brings blessings!

"Then the Lord said, 'I have pardoned [them] according to your word; [but] ...THEY CERTAINLY SHALL NOT SEE THE LAND OF WHICH I SWORE TO THEIR FATHERS, NOR SHALL ANY OF THOSE WHO REJECTED ME SEE IT. YOU [MOSES] SHALL BY NO MEANS enter the land [either]...'" (Numbers 14:20,23,30b). What a sad day this was for Moses. As a type of husband, he dearly loved his wife. But no matter how deep our love is for those we are intimately connected with, our love for God must be first and foremost; otherwise we are in idolatry. It's a decision to trust the Lord. If we will not break a relationship when God shows us to do so, we're in sin; our life will come to a standstill until we obey, or until we die.

THERE'S STILL HOPE

The tragedy or blessedness of our life results from the choices that we have or have not made. Even though we may have made serious errors, our God is a God of hope, of comfort, and of great mercy. But He MUST have our cooperation. When we attempt to do life our way, it is NOT cooperation. It is rebellion. Yes, we do miss out on what God has prepared for us.

Thankfully, He is very gracious to give us another plan and to help us start again. He delights in giving us a new start. It takes a tough decision to serve Him faithfully NO MATTER WHAT.

The Lord Jesus was resting on a well when He had an encounter with a woman who had apparently given up (See John 4:5-39). Her life was a mess. She'd had five husbands already. Afraid to have another failed marriage she chose to live with the sixth man. It was too difficult for her to make another "to death do us part" commitment. She may have felt she had to protect herself by not getting too involved — no strings attached.

When she went that day to draw water from the well, her life was changed. She came face to face with God. Jesus told her He knew about her failed marriages and the man she lived with. But right where she was, Jesus offered her a new life in Him.

After a life changing experience with Jesus the woman left and ran back to the city to tell the others of the good news. Meanwhile, Jesus' disciples urged Him to eat. However, Jesus' mind was still on the woman. He knew that the work that was given to Him by His heavenly Father was to reach out to this woman and others like her (See John 4:18-34). Jesus is still reaching out. His work is not finished until all have the opportunity to come back.

2

MARRYING OUTSIDE THE WILL OF GOD

MARRYING OUTSIDE THE WILL OF GOD CAN DESTROY A NATION

God used divorce to break up marriage relationships in order to SAVE a nation. Does he also use divorce to save us from a wrong or bad marriage so ALL is not lost? Yes!

Israel, the apple of God's eye, was a mighty nation. They served a mighty God. Before they crossed the Red Sea with Moses, they were numbered at *"...about six hundred thousand men on foot, besides children" (Exodus 12:37)*. The 600,000 people did not include the women, children, and those who rode on camel, horse, or donkey. It is estimated that between four to seven million people crossed the Red Sea in that day. What a great number of people, what a large nation.

But something happened. Between the years 1491 B.C. and 457 B.C., the children of Israel were on their way to extinction. No more are they a great nation, but only "a remnant." Instead of four to seven million people, *"The whole assembly together was forty-two thousand three hundred and sixty..." (Ezra 2:64)*. The population of the nation of Israel dropped over 99% during this time.

Even though Israel was a mighty nation, because of disobedience they were attacked, overcome, and taken captive to the nation of Babylon. God continued to bless them even while they were in captivity. Nevertheless, they still chose to do their own thing. They blamed others and other things for all their problems. Even after their time of Babylonian captivity had ended, their population kept dropping because they had not made their hearts right with God.

Through Divine intervention, the people of Israel were released to go home. Sadly, they still did not uphold the commandments of the Lord. How much do we have to go through before we realize that God's commandments are given to keep us from unnecessary suffering?

The people continued in disobedience after returning to their own land. They did not follow the Lord's commands concerning marriage. Again, their nation that had been reduced to 42,360 people was in jeopardy. [1]

"...By profaning the covenant of the fathers ...An abomination has been committed in Israel and in Jerusalem, for JUDAH HAS PROFANED THE LORD'S HOLY INSTITUTION [MARRIAGE] which He loves: HE HAS MARRIED THE DAUGHTER OF A FOREIGN GOD. May the Lord cut off from the tents of Jacob the man who does this, yet you say, 'for what reason?' Because the Lord has been witness between you and the wife of your youth, with whom you have dealt treacherously; yet she is your companion and the wife by covenant. But did he not make them one...? And why one? HE SEEKS GODLY OFFSPRING" (Malachi 2:10c,11,12a,14,15a-c).

That's what God wants — a godly offspring. Godly people walk in righteousness. For *"righteousness exalts a nation, but sin is a reproach to any people"* (Proverbs 14:34. This sin had such deep consequences that the whole fabric of the nation was eroding. The only thing that could stop the deterioration of families and the nation was divorce. Ezra the prophet tells the story:

Ezra said that God's people *"HAVE NOT SEPARATED THEMSELVES from the peoples of ...the Canaanites, Hittites, Perizzites, Jebusites, Ammonites, Moabites, Egyptians, and Amorites. For THEY have taken [them] as wives ...in this wicked act and direct violation [of God's will]"* (Ezra 9:1-2 AMP). They joined with these people in all manner of business and social activity, including marriage. Those in leadership were the worst violators of God's will in this matter.

Ezra said, *"...O my God, I am ashamed and blush to lift my face to you, my God, for our iniquities have risen higher than our heads and our guilt has mounted to the heavens ...and for OUR WILLFULNESS we, our kings, and our priests have been delivered into the hands of the kings of the lands, to the sword, captivity, plundering, and utter shame ...And now, for a brief moment, GRACE has been shown us by the Lord our God..."* (Ezra 9:6-8 AMP).

Notice that the "grace" that was shown by the Lord was the ability to separate and divorce the wives they married

38

outside of God's will. For they *"...have committed the abominations ...[of the] peoples of the lands" (Ezra 9:1, AMP).* Doesn't this "grace" to separate sound like the "peace" to separate, given by God in 1Corinthians 7:15? *"But if the unbeliever departs, let him depart; a brother or sister IS NOT UNDER BONDAGE IN SUCH CASES. But God has called us to PEACE."*

"And now, for a brief moment, GRACE HAS BEEN SHOWN US by the Lord our God, who has left us a remnant TO ESCAPE and has given us a secure hold in His holy place..." (Ezra 9:8 AMP). It is God's heart toward man to provide a way of escape from a bad situation and into His mercy. The provision for divorce was not for them to escape FROM God's will, but was an escape from being OUT of His will, and an escape back INTO His will.

"...For the people wept bitterly" (Ezra 10:1b AMP). This was not a matter to consider lightly. They knew that families were going to break up. They knew that those they had grown to love would soon be cast forth from the family. This was a hard thing, but they had to do it. If they didn't, their nation would be lost. Their families would be separated from the blessings and covenants of God. The seed of Christ could not be preserved through a holy bloodline. Hardship and distress would be their lot.

So they said, *"We have broken faith and dealt treacherously against our God and have married foreign women of the peoples of the land; yet now there is STILL HOPE for Israel in spite of this thing" (Ezra 10:2b AMP).* Yes, there was "still hope," but the hope of God was for them to return to the place where He originally wanted them, separated and divorced from the peoples of that land. This is why it is so important to know God's heart. He is the One who instituted marriage, the One who "joins together" and who "brings a sword" to divide.

As the Israelites repented, they found hope. With this hope, they said, *"Therefore, let us MAKE A COVENANT WITH OUR GOD TO PUT AWAY [SEPARATE WITHOUT GIVING A CERTIFICATE OF DIVORCE] all the foreign wives and their children, according to the ...command of our God. Arise, FOR IT IS YOUR DUTY ...be strong and brave and do it!" (Ezra 10:3,4 AMP).*

39

When the command came forth from God to divorce their foreign wives and their children, Ezra knew the pain that would be involved. That is why he said to them, "be strong and brave and do it!" *"Then Ezra ...made ...all Israel swear that they would do as had been said. ...Ezra ...ate no bread and drank no water, for he mourned..." (Ezra 10:5,6 AMP)*. It is not easy to correct a difficult situation. Neither is it easy to tell someone to do it.

"And a proclamation was made ...that they should assemble in Jerusalem ...that whoever did not come within three days ...all his property should be forfeited and he himself BANNED FROM THE ASSEMBLY [CHURCH]" (Ezra 10:8 AMP). Imagine, people would actually be kicked out of church for NOT divorcing their spouse.

"...And all the people sat in the open space before the house of God, trembling because of this matter..." (Ezra 10:9 AMP). God is looking for and purifying a people who will walk with Him. The cry of our Father God is to have a family, a holy family, a loving family, and a family who honors their Father!

"And Ezra the priest ...said to them, you have acted wickedly ...and have married foreign women ...So now make confession and give thanks to the Lord, AND DO HIS WILL. SEPARATE YOURSELVES from the peoples of the land and from [your] foreign heathen wives. Then all the assembly answered with a loud voice, as you have said, so must we do. But the people are many ...Nor can this work be done in a day or two, for we have greatly transgressed in this matter ...let all in our cities who have foreign wives come by appointment ...UNTIL THE FIERCE WRATH OF OUR GOD OVER THIS MATTER IS TURNED FROM US" (Ezra 10:10-14 AMP).

So *"...Ezra the priest and certain heads ...sat down on the first day of the tenth month to investigate the matter. [When] they had come to the end of the cases of the men married to foreign wives.... THEY SOLEMNLY VOWED TO PUT AWAY [SEPARATED FROM] THEIR WIVES, and, being guilty, [each] offered a ram of the flock for [his] guilt" (Ezra 10:16,17,19 AMP)*.

Ezra 2:64-65 reveals that there was 42,360 people left of Israel. Those who were married to native heathen women numbered only 17 priests, 10 Levites, and 86 laymen - 113 in all, according to the records. [1] Because 113 men decided to do what they wanted to do with THEIR marriage by marrying outside of God's will, 42,360 people suffered.

We often think that our actions have no affect on anyone else. Perhaps we think that we're insignificant or a self-made person. This is not the case. Every person belongs to a family. The nation is made up of many families. What happens in our families, ALWAYS affects others.

GOD'S USE OF DIVORCE IS TO *SAVE*, NOT DESTROY

Does God hate ALL divorce? No. He knows the ONLY way to bring a holy people out of a people, is to "separate." This is the only way God can preserve a remnant of the people for a holy family unto Himself.

We may think that God's command to divorce their foreign wives was terrible. However, look at it with God's eyes. Certainly, God sees the pain of the "one family" going through this separating process, but He also sees the much greater pain of the innocent ones of the nation suffering from the sins of the few. We're talking about only 113 marriages outside the will of God, causing a nation to be on the verge of being wiped out. Now that's devastation! Let us not think that God hates us, even after we have done wrong. He is much greater than our sin. But He will require us to get back on track with Him. For the Scriptures truly say, *"My son, do not despise the chastening of the Lord, nor detest His correction; FOR WHOM THE LORD LOVES HE CORRECTS, just as a father the son in whom he delights"* (Proverbs 3:11,12).

Many times we get into situations that are not the will of God. If we will simply be honest with ourselves, most of the time we know it's wrong but we want to do it anyway. We didn't end up in the situation overnight and it may take more time than we realize to unravel the years of entanglement. Keep in mind what the Lord did when He drove out the inhabitants of the Promised

Land that He was giving to the people of Israel to inhabit. He said, *"I will not drive them out from before you in one year, lest [so that not] the land become desolate and the beasts of the field become too numerous for you. LITTLE BY LITTLE I will drive them out from before you, UNTIL YOU HAVE INCREASED, and you inherit the land"* (Exodus 23:29-30).

We may be looking for an overnight miracle, but God's normal process is "little by little" until we have increased.

MARRYING OUTSIDE YOUR RACE

"Did you know that most science books say there are at least four races of humans — and that these books are all wrong? A scientist, speaking at a recent American Association for The Advancement of Science Convention, gives the correct answer about 'Race': 'Race is a social construct derived mainly from perceptions conditioned by events of recorded history, and it has no basic biological reality.' What this person is saying is that, biologically, there is only *one* race of human beings. After all, all humans are classified as *'Homo Sapiens.'"* [2]

For *"God, who made the world and everything in it, since He is Lord of heaven and earth ...He gives to all life, breath, and all things. AND HE MADE FROM ONE BLOOD [FROM ONE PERSON, ADAM] EVERY NATION [EVERY ETHNIC GROUP] OF MEN TO DWELL ON ALL THE FACE OF THE EARTH..."* (Acts 17: 24-26).

THEREFORE, A "RACE" IS CORRECTLY DEFINED AS AN "ETHNIC GROUP — A PEOPLE WHO HOLD TO A PARTICULAR CULTURE," NOT A CLASS OF PEOPLE, OR A PEOPLE WITH A PECULIAR LOOK, OR A DIFFERENT SKIN COLOR. The Lord made from one person, every nation. Actually, the word "nation" in the Greek text means "ethnic group." A race is not the people themselves, but their ethnic group — their culture. You can have two of any color of the same people, and have different races — ethnic groups. That is the way it is at this moment around this world, and it has been like this from the beginning of time. Our own prejudices have twisted it.

No bloodline is pure. Not even the Lord Jesus, who was from the tribe of Judah, a Jew, had a pure bloodline. He had swindlers, murders and prostitutes in His linage. **GOD'S DESIRE IS TO HAVE DIFFERENT CULTURES, NOT PURE BLOODLINES.**

Now that "race" has been correctly defined, let's look further into marrying outside of one's race.

Some say that the race of a person is done away with regarding marriage to those who are born again in Christ — it doesn't matter who one marries. The race of a person is done away with concerning being born again into the family of God, but not concerning marriage. Let me explain:

The Scripture says that in Christ *"There is neither Jew nor Greek ...there is neither male nor female..." (Galatians 3:28).* There are no ethnic or gender barriers. ALL who have become children of God through the shed blood of Christ have the same covenantal rights in the family of God, according to the portion that Christ gives to each one. This is God's plan: to have a many-membered, many-cultured body, not only in the Body of Christ, but also in all of society. God's call has gone out, that *"...WHOEVER calls on the name of the Lord shall be saved" (Romans 10:13).*

If this Scripture, Galatians 3:28, which says, *"There is neither Jew nor Greek ...THERE IS NEITHER MALE NOR FEMALE..."* were true regarding marriage and marrying outside one's race, then the part that says, *"there is neither male nor female"* must apply to the marriage partners also, meaning, male can marry male and female can marry female. In seeing this, we know that this Scripture cannot and does not pertain to marriage, because God hates the practice of homosexuality. He says that those men who are *"...leaving the natural use of the woman, burned in their lust for one another, men with men committing what is shameful, AND RECEIVING IN THEMSELVES THE PENALTY OF THEIR ERROR WHICH WAS DUE... who knowing the righteous judgment of God, that THOSE WHO PRACTICE SUCH THINGS ARE DESERVING OF DEATH..." (Romans 1:27,32).* But as far as the race of a person is in the church, it has been done away with in Christ. There are no barriers to who our brother and sister are in the Lord. For *"...[we] are ALL ONE in Christ Jesus" (Galatians 3:28b).*

43

Notice how nature operates. The animal kingdom breeds with its own kind. Birds do not pair up and breed out of their own kind: sparrows mate with sparrows, blue jays with blue jays, finches with finches and cardinals with cardinals. They know their own kind. The sparrow doesn't say, "I'm going to hot-tail-it over to the cardinal's nest and spend the night." No, they mate with their own kind. They all have different song languages; their feather dress is different; their very mannerisms are different. What a variety and what beauty God has designed.

If all birds crossbred, we would have one kind of bird. That means there would be no bird-watchers, no beauty in the varieties of nest building, no flashy colors or variety of song, and no Discovery Channel to see all the variations of God's creation at the click of a button. **THE *DIFFERENCES* OF EVERYTHING THAT GOD HAS CREATED *IS THE BEAUTY OF CREATION*.** We are to embrace the beauty of each other's differences. NOT to try to conform others to "our" beauty.

God loves diversity. He created diversity. This diversity is not only in the plant, animal, and fish world, but also of the people of the earth who are the crown of His creation and the affection of His heart!

In summary:

A "species" is properly defined as a category or grouping of a plant, animal, or living thing. Do not be confused. A "race" is NOT a species. A "race" is the same as a culture or ethnic group. The old saying, "stick with your own *kind*" speaks of cultural differences.

Color has absolutely no bearing on the matter of marriage. Man sees from the "outward" appearance and consequently judges others from what he sees. All racism comes from pride or fear. Pride because they believe they are better, fear because they are afraid of the unknown.

God wants a many-membered many-cultured body. That is what makes the beauty of this world in spite of what some people may think.

God has always brought people from one culture into another. That is what a missionary is. He has always said to accept strangers (other cultures) as your own family when they "adopt" (my word) Him and His culture as their own. The general rule is that the culture should always grow within itself. However, He has always brought people from one culture to be apart of another whether it is through marriage or not. And that happens every day. It is just not the "general" rule.

CHRIST: MANY-MEMBERED, MANY-CULTURED, EACH DISTINCT

God WANTS a many-membered, many-cultured body with each part being unique in itself. This is not racism. This is unity in diversity. A body has members that look differently, act differently, and function differently. Whoever heard of a hand rebelling against the feet, saying, "I want to be like you. I want to have the same rights and wear those shoes you wear. I want to do the walking for a change!" Whoever heard of such a silly idea? Yet, to a large degree in the church this foolishness is accepted as truth. Our physical body and Christ's body is MANY membered with each member being DIFFERENT.

As I was driving one day in the wee hours of the morning, the Lord started speaking to my heart regarding relationships using similarities between the human physical body and His many-membered, many-cultured body on earth, the body of Christ. Two of the things He said were:

(1) "There are certain things one part of the body will do for another part, but that part will NEVER do it back. Like, the hands will go and scratch the feet, but the feet will probably never scratch the hands, nor are they designed to. So it is in Christ's body, one member (a person, ministry, or culture of people) may do something for another member, but that member may never do it back, nor should it be expected to."

(2) "The different sections of the body live in different environments, each part being distinct. As the feet are usually

covered up, they are hot. The face is exposed. So it is in the body of Christ; these are different cultures, nations of people: each distinct in itself."

Now, this is nothing new. The Scripture tells us we are different (See 1Corinthians 12:14-26). However, using this analogy, what if each member of the physical body married another part. Pretty soon the offspring would look nothing like the original member. Moreover, if there were enough cross-marriages, then the "many-membered" body would no longer exist. It would become a "member" in itself. God does do that when he forms a new nation, a new member, out of a few nations. But these are seasonal things that He does through the ages. I'll speak more on this later. God does not want to do away with a many-membered, many-cultured body. He wants the body to function in its uniqueness and completeness.

"FOR IN FACT THE BODY IS NOT ONE MEMBER BUT MANY. If the foot should say, 'because I am not a hand, I am not of the body,' is it therefore not of the body? And if the ear should say, 'because I am not an eye, I am not of the body,' is it therefore not of the body? If the whole body were an eye, where would be the hearing? If the whole were hearing, where would be the smelling? But now God has set the members, each one of them, in the body just as He pleased. AND IF THEY WERE ALL ONE MEMBER, WHERE WOULD THE BODY BE? But now indeed there are many members, yet one body" (1Corinthians 12:14-20).

THE RACES OF PEOPLES AND THE BLESSINGS OF GOD

Since the race of a person is not done away with in marriage, then what's the significance of being distinct and marrying within your own ethnic group?

In Ezra 10:11, God's people married outside of their own race and tribe. They found themselves separated from God's purpose and connected to a people of a different purpose. For this reason God told them to *"...SEPARATE YOURSELVES from* the peoples of the land..." (Ezra 10:11). When two unlikes are connected together, the Scripture tells us that we are "unequally yoked" (See 2Corinthians 6:14-15). A Christian should not marry a non-Christian; but let's say they were both Christians from two different races.

All races of people go back to Noah, his three sons and their families, the survivors of the world flood, and from there the line goes back to Adam. The names of Noah's sons are Shem, Ham, and Japheth (See Genesis 7:13). **FOR IT IS NOT THE RACE ITSELF, OR OF WHICH SIDE OF THE FAMILY OF NOAH WE MARRY INTO, BUT IT'S THE BLESSINGS AND CURSINGS, GIFTS AND CALLINGS THAT ARE SPECIFIC TO A CERTAIN FAMILY LINEAGE.** We can see this from Noah to his sons and offspring from which all nations (ethnic groups) have their beginning.

The blessings and cursing to (one of Ham's sons), Canaan, were:

Noah said, *"...cursed be Canaan [Ham's son]; a servant of servants he [the nations from Ham's son] shall be to his brethren [the other nations]"* (Genesis 9:25).

The clans and tribes from the seed of Ham moved southward. The names given Ham's descendants are similar to those of land areas in Central Arabia, Egypt, the east shore of the Mediterranean Sea and the eastern coast of Africa. Interestingly, Egypt was once called "The land of Ham" and the name of an early pagan God of Egypt was a transliteration of the name Ham. [3]

The blessings and cursing to Shem were:

"...blessed be the Lord, the God of Shem, and may Canaan [the nations from Ham's son] be His servant" (Genesis 9:26).

Shem's descendants stayed closer to the Middle East and made up the central nations of the eastern hemisphere. The Bible gives us the genealogy from Shem to Abraham, the father of the Jews. Most of those who are fighting in the Middle East in modern times are truly all members of the Semitic tribes. Arabs and Israelis are both Semites. Arabic nations have sprung from

Abraham's son Ishmael while Israel consists of descendants of Abraham through Isaac and Jacob. [4]

As far as the Jews are concerned, it is commonly believed that they are a race within themselves. But that is not the case. The Jewish people themselves are of different races — different ethnic groups, depending in which part of the world they live and the type of culture they adopt. The Scriptures bear this out by telling of a *"just man, and one that feared God, and of good report among ALL THE NATIONS (ETHNIC GROUPS) OF THE JEWS" (Acts 10:22).* Just because people are of the same origin, does not mean that they are of the same race — the same ethnic group. Race is far beyond color or looks. It's culture! This is the norm over the earth.

The blessings and cursing to Japheth were:

"May God enlarge Japheth, and may He dwell in the tents of Shem; and may Canaan be His servant" (Genesis 9:27).

The tribal group that grew from Japheth's seed moved northward and settled in regions around the Black and Caspian Seas. Their descendants became the Caucasian races of Europe and Asia, including the natives of North America who probably crossed the Bering Straits from Asia and moved southward to warmer climates in the Western Hemisphere. [5]

Those powerful prophetic words spoken by Noah set the course of the nations to come. Whether these blessings and cursing were the will of God remains to be known. For it is still given unto man by God to *"...have dominion...on the earth" (Genesis 1:26).* The Scripture says, that *"The heaven, even the heavens, are the Lord's; But the earth He has given to the children of men" (Psalm 115:16).*

If we look at the nations of the world today, a picture of Noah's words is what we see. The issue is not whether Noah was right or wrong in what he prophesied, but that he did speak it into existence.

Thankfully, when a person becomes a member of God's family, they do not have to live under the curses anymore. Nevertheless, the different cultures are still set by God. God

"...has made from one blood every nation of men to dwell on all the face of the earth, and has DETERMINED THEIR PREAPPOINTED TIMES AND THE BOUNDARIES OF THEIR DWELLINGS, so that they should seek the Lord...and find Him..." (Acts 17:26-27).

We can even see the blessings and curses broken down even further in the nations of Shem. Abraham, a descendant of Shem, received a very special blessing pronounced on him and his descendants by God Himself. God said, *"blessings I will bless you, and multiplying I will multiply your descendants as the stars of the heaven and as the sand which is on the seashore; and your descendants shall possess the gate of their enemies. IN YOUR SEED (who is Jesus Christ) ALL THE NATIONS (ETHNIC GROUPS) OF THE EARTH SHALL BE BLESSED..."* (Genesis 22:17,18). Jesus, who is of the linage of Abraham, came to earth to bring salvation to all ethnic groups because one man dared to believe and obey God.

KEEPING THE BLESSINGS FOR AN APPOINTED GENERATION

Keep in mind that the problem is not the race we marry into, BUT THE APPOINTMENT FOR THAT RACE: God's specific purpose for them to play in the history of the earth. Now let's look at a problem that arose between the twelve tribes of Israel. They were marrying outside their own tribe.

God planned that the tribes would become nations. This is what He promised Abraham. God had specific appointments for each nation. The command of the Lord was to *"let them marry whom they think best, but they may marry ONLY within the family of their father's tribe. SO THE INHERITANCE OF THE CHILDREN OF ISRAEL SHALL NOT CHANGE HANDS FROM TRIBE TO TRIBE [OR NATION TO NATION], for everyone of the children of Israel shall keep the inheritance of the tribe [nation] of his fathers. THUS, NO INHERITANCE SHALL CHANGE HANDS from one tribe [nation] to another, but every tribe [nation] of the children of Israel shall keep its own inheritance"* (Numbers 36:6-9).

Marrying within our own kind has nothing to do with loving or not loving someone else. It has much to do with receiving God's best for our families, and assuring that God's best will not end with us, but will flow down to future generations as God has predestined. If there were a marriage between different tribes, the inheritance (blessing) would leave that tribe and enter another; hence, future generations lost out (See Numbers 36:3).

Some may say that these Scriptures don't apply because we are in the New Covenant under grace and the Old Covenant of the law is passed away. Thank God we are under grace, but so was Adam and Abraham and Moses. The Old Covenant (Testament) is just as much grace as the New Covenant (Testament). And the New Covenant is just as much law as the Old Covenant. What makes the difference is when we yield our hearts up to the Holy Spirit and allow Him to lead our life; He gives us power to walk in accordance with the Bible. Otherwise, we fail because ALL the Scriptures become law and void of life. For *"...the letter [of the Old and New Testaments themselves] kills, but the Spirit [Himself] gives life [to BOTH Old and New Covenants]" (2Corinthians 3:6)*. He, the Spirit of God, makes the word of God "alive in our hearts" (See also, John 6:63, Hebrews 4:12).

Ephesians 2:12,13 tells us we are no longer *"...strangers from the COVENANTS of promise...."* Not just one covenant, the New Covenant, but COVENANTS, Old and New. Since we are no longer strangers of the blessings of both covenants because we keep God's commandments, then also, we are no longer strangers of the curses of both covenants if we violate and disregard God's commands.

GENERAL LAW, SPECIAL LAW

There are strategic times when God makes allowances for what I will call His "general law." God reserves the right to supersede general law by what I will call His "special law." These general scriptural laws are given to all of God's children. If we do not obey God's law, it's sin. But there are times when God specifically overrides a specific law or command to reveal and unveil a certain condition, or to do a new thing in the earth. **HENCE, SPECIAL LAW OVERRIDES GENERAL LAW.**

For example, the Lord told Hosea the prophet to *"GO, TAKE YOURSELF A WIFE OF HARLOTRY and [have] children of harlotry..." (Hosea 1:2b).* Yet, the Lord speaking through the apostle Paul said, *"Do you not know that your bodies are members of Christ? Shall I then take the members of Christ and make them members of a harlot? Certainly not! Or do you not know that HE WHO IS JOINED TO A HARLOT IS ONE BODY WITH HER? FLEE sexual immorality.... therefore glorify God in your body..." (1Corinthians 6:15-16a,18a,20).* What happened? Why did God say to one person to join with a prostitute and on the other hand tell us not to be joined to a prostitute? It's because special law overrode general law.

God told Hosea to marry a harlot and make her his wife, not just to use her as a harlot. The Scriptures bear out that she had harlotry in her heart. And even though married, she had sexual relations with others. For she was the example of what was in the hearts of God's people. Hosea's wife conceived three times, but there is no mention of who the father was (See Hosea 1:3,6,8,9). We know only what God said to the people of Israel, *"I will not have mercy on her children, FOR THEY ARE THE CHILDREN OF HARLOTRY. For their mother has played the harlot; she who conceived them has behaved shamefully. For she said, 'I will go after my lovers...'" (Hosea 2:4,5).*

Even though 2Corinthians 6:14 says not to be "unequally yoked together," that was the very point that God wanted to reveal to His people. The once-intimate relationship that joined God and His people was gone; they left their first love. They were whoring around with other gods.

Their inheritance in the kingdom of God was in jeopardy: *"...For the land has committed great harlotry by departing from the Lord" (Hosea 1:2b).* God had his prophet who loved Him with all his heart, bear the very sin that His people were committing. God overrode His command of "not-to-do," by commanding Hosea "to-do" that which He said generally not to do. God did this to reveal to them that they are doing the very thing He commanded them not to do. The very sin that separated them

51

from God, God used as a call to repentance and restoration. For it is truly written, *"...that ALL THINGS work together for good to those who love God..." (Romans 8:28a).*

Here's another example of God overriding His general law with His special law. This deals with an interracial marriage that was appointed and approved by God Himself. It was the marriage of Moses and his second wife, an Ethiopian woman. She was a Cushite, from Ham's son Cush, who is Noah's grandson. Incidentally, Egypt is called "the Land of Ham" (See Psalms 105:23-38).

The Bible does not say what happened to Moses' first wife, whether she died or that they were divorced, but only that he remarried.

Many times it has been thought that Moses fell in love with this Ethiopian woman and went off and married her without regard to God's law, the people he ruled, his brother Aaron or his sister Miriam. The Bible does say, *"...in the multitude of (wise) counselors there is safety" (Proverbs 11:14b).* But as always, there is a balance. The Bible also states regarding God and His people, *"My sheep hear MY VOICE, and I know them, and they FOLLOW ME. ...For they do not know the voice of strangers" (John 10:27,5).* Here lies the problem. Jesus said, "My sheep know my voice," no matter whether His voice comes out of the mouth of a person, a book, a revelation, the Bible or with whatever method God chooses to use to speak to our hearts.

When we ask for wisdom and direction from someone when making a decision, and our hearts do not recognize the voice as the voice of God, then it's the voice of a stranger and we *"...will by no means follow..." (John 10:5);* even if it's spoken from the mouth of our closest relatives, like Aaron and Miriam spoke to their brother, Moses, we must not follow.

His *"[sister] Miriam and [his brother] Aaron spoke against Moses because of the Ethiopian woman whom he had married; for he had married an Ethiopian woman" (Numbers 12:1).* The Scriptures imply that Aaron and Miriam both told their brother Moses that the LORD told them that he married outside the will of God and that he should divorce her. *"So they said, 'Has the*

Lord indeed spoken ONLY through Moses? Has He not spoken through us [Aaron and Miriam] ALSO?'" (Numbers 12:2). If Moses had married within his race, he would have been OUT of the will of God.

We have to be very careful when taking advice from anyone. Their voice MUST be recognized by the written Word of God, and in our heart as "the voice of God."

So as Moses and his brother and sister were engaged in this marriage dispute, *"The Lord heard it. [And] suddenly the Lord said to Moses, Aaron, and Miriam, 'Come out, you three, to the Tabernacle of Meeting!' So the three came out. Then the Lord came down in the pillar of cloud and stood in the door of the Tabernacle, and called Aaron and Miriam. And they both went forward"* (Numbers 12:2c,4,5). God was angry! He was about ready to give Aaron and Miriam a royal reaming they would never forget. When God calls us to front and center, it's serious business.

"Then He said, 'Hear now MY words: if there is a prophet among you, [which Miriam was (See Exodus 15:20)] I, the Lord, make myself known to him in a vision; I speak to him in a dream. NOT SO WITH MY SERVANT MOSES; He is faithful in all My house. I SPEAK WITH HIM FACE TO FACE, plainly and not in dark sayings" (Numbers 12:6-8a). The next few verses tell how angry God was with Miriam and Aaron for prying into Moses' marriage, and how God struck Miriam with leprosy and how Moses cried out to God in Miriam's behalf and He healed her.

(The Scriptures reveal that God is NEVER angry with us since the death and resurrection of His Son Jesus. Jesus, with His own blood satisfied the claims that sin had against man, and satisfied the pain in God's heart because of sinful man.)

The next two important points establish the fact that Moses did not marry outside of his race on his own accord, but it was a marriage that God desired to bring about for a purpose. First, *"The man Moses was very humble, MORE THAN ALL THE MEN WHO WERE ON THE FACE OF THE EARTH"* (Numbers 12:3). Second, God spoke to Moses "FACE TO FACE." When a person is more humble than anyone else in the world, and is one to whom God speaks face to face, we KNOW that they talk with God about ALL their affairs, especially marriage.

DIFFERENT MEMBERS *ARE* THE PLAN

I said all that to say this: God is not a racist! He is the Creator! He created DIFFERENT races TO BE DIFFERENT. Each group of people with their own culture is a different member of society, making up the whole. *"But now God has set the members, each one of them, in the body just as HE pleased. AND IF THEY WERE ALL ONE MEMBER, WHERE WOULD THE BODY BE?" (1Corinthians 12:18,19).*

In 1822, Cornplanter, a half-breed Indian chief of the Seneca Nation, while addressing the Warren County courthouse to protest the taxation of his land by the state of Pennsylvania, had this to say: "The Great Spirit bids me tell the white people... The white people have broken his command, by mixing their color with the Indians. The Indians have done better by not doing so." [6]

The "white" people Cornplanter were talking about were actually represented by a number of cultures or races — the French, English, Scottish, etc. though he may not have known it. Their color and features are what distinguished Cornplanter's people from the "white" people, even though his people and the white people are from the same descendent, Japheth, Noah's son.

The proper terminology for "interracial marriage" is intercultural marriage. Intercultural marriages are destined by God at preappointed times to create a new member of society, NOT to cause all the different members to become one member.

If we were a building designer, how would we like it if we designed a major structure and during the building process, someone continually went about making their own changes to the plans? Nothing would be built correctly.

God is the Master Designer. He is the Designer of the world and the different functions of the peoples. HE has the master plans; we don't. In His divine purpose, He's planned to use specific nationalities at predestinated times in the future only to find out they have become a different people because of intermarriages. The original blessings, gifts and anointing to accomplish the predestined tasks no longer exist; they were transferred out of the nation and the portion designated to another nation was transferred in. Thus, a mal-prepared and mal-equipped people were formed who are unable to fulfill the preappointed plan for God's intended purposes.

There are still things we do not know regarding this subject, but God knows. If we will diligently inquire for His direction, He will show us the way. **REMEMBER, COLOR OR FACIAL FEATURES DO NOT MAKE UP A RACE, BUT CULTURE DOES.**

3

THE RIGHT TO DIVORCE

WHO INVENTED DIVORCE ANYWAY?

Many times, we think unconsciously that MAN came up with the idea of divorce. We figured that after the fall of man in the Garden of Eden, man, who was now spiritually separated from his Maker, couldn't deal anymore with the pressures of the marriage. So man came up with the idea of divorce. Not so.

God knew what was in the heart of man before He ever created him. He knows the "beginning and the end." He knew man was going to need a savior. He knew that savior was going to be His only Son. And He foreknew that because of the sin nature now in man, there would not only be divorce, but the NEED for divorce. God Himself had that need.

There was a time when God actually divorced His mate. *"Then I saw that for all the causes for which backsliding Israel had committed adultery, I had PUT HER AWAY [SEPARATED FROM HER] AND given her a CERTIFICATE OF DIVORCE..."* *(Jeremiah. 3:8).*

"Thus says the Lord: 'WHERE IS the certificate of your mother's divorce, WHOM I HAVE PUT AWAY [SEPARATED FROM]? For your iniquities you have sold yourselves, and for your transgressions your mother has been put away'" (Isaiah 50:1a,c). In this instance, God only "put her away"— had a legal separation but not a divorce. That is why He said, "WHERE IS the certificate of your mothers divorce?"

There were times God commanded His people to separate from (without giving a certificate of divorce) their mates so they wouldn't be carried off with their spouses' rebellion. *"Now therefore, make confession to the Lord God of your fathers, and DO HIS WILL; SEPARATE YOURSELVES from the peoples of the land, and FROM PAGAN WIVES" (Ezra 10:11).*

Also, *"You shall not give your daughters as wives to their sons, nor take their daughters for your sons or yourselves. Did not Solomon king of Israel sin by these things? Yet among many nations there was no king like him, who was beloved of his God; and God made him king over all Israel. NEVERTHELESS pagan women caused EVEN HIM TO SIN. Should we then hear of your* doings all this great evil, *TRANSGRESSING AGAINST OUR GOD BY MARRYING PAGAN WOMEN? Thus I cleansed them of EVERYTHING pagan"* (Nehemiah 13:25b-27,30a).

The Scriptures say that Jesus came to set the captives free, not to keep them bound (See Isaiah 61:1, Luke 4:18). A person can be just as bound by the sin nature of a spouse lording it over them, as one can be by the power of drugs, alcohol, or any other destructive vice.

Divorce and remarriage was never a question with God. For *"When a man takes a wife and marries her, and it happens that she finds no favor in his eyes because he has found some uncleanness in her, AND HE WRITES HER A CERTIFICATE OF DIVORCE, puts it in her hand and sends her out of his house, and goes AND BECOMES ANOTHER MAN'S WIFE..."* (Deuteronomy 24:1,2). The "certificate of divorce" was the wife's GUARANTEE to be able to get remarried.

And again, *"Are you bound to a wife? Do not seek to be loosed. Are you LOOSED FROM A WIFE? Do not seek a wife. BUT EVEN IF YOU DO MARRY, YOU HAVE NOT SINNED"* (1Corinthians 7:27,28a).

There were times when God forbids His people to divorce. There are two situations in Deuteronomy 22:13-30 where God has REMOVED the right to divorce. This means that when needed, the right to divorce has always been there. In these cases that right was abused, so God revoked it. The first instance was when the husband claimed that his new wife was not a virgin, when in fact, she was proved to be so. Because the husband brought a bad name on her, *"...He cannot divorce her all his days"* (Deuteronomy 22:19b).

The other case was when a man had sex with a single woman who was a virgin. He must pay support money (the dowry of a bride) to her family, and by having sex with her he has taken her as his wife and *"...[Was not] permitted to divorce her all his days"* (Deuteronomy 22:29b). But *"if her father utterly refuses to give her to him [the marriage would be cancelled and father and daughter would keep the dowry]"* (Exodus 22:16).

The right to divorce has always existed, but in these cases, that right was lost. **THUS, GOD RECOGNIZES THE NEED FOR DIVORCE, FOR HIMSELF AND FOR MAN.**

Divorce, as a method to separate marriages, can be used like any other method, for good or evil. When methods are used for evil, we tend to shy away from them. However, when they are used for good, we tend to give them honor. The difficult part of this is when a method has been used in an evil way, pronounced to be evil, taught to be evil, and then recommended to be used and accepted as good; the minds of the people are so conditioned at this point, that there is an immediate rejection. This is the primary reason for this teaching on divorce. God Himself is setting the record straight.

GOD HATES MARRIAGE?

Have you ever heard anyone say, "God hates marriage?" Of course not! Have you ever heard anyone say, "God hates divorce?" Sure we have, especially when they are not the ones faced with that dilemma. The phrase, "God hates divorce" has been used against married couples as a blanket answer to cover all types of marriage problems. As we will find out from God's Word, that is just not true. Neither is it true that God hates marriage. On the contrary, God is the one who instituted marriage between a man and a woman. *"Therefore a man shall leave his father and mother and be joined to his wife, and they shall become one flesh" (Genesis 2:24).*

Even though God instituted marriage, He does not approve of ALL marriages. This can be clearly seen in the lives of the people of Israel written in Ezra, chapter 9 and 10, and Deuteronomy 7:15. In Ezra, God disapproved of the marriages and His judgment was on them until they corrected the situation by divorcing their spouses and even separating from their children that were born from those marriages. In Deuteronomy, God said, *"NOR SHALL YOU MAKE MARRIAGES WITH THEM. For they will turn your sons away from following Me" (Deuteronomy 7:3,4).* In this situation, these are the marriages that God hates.

We can also see that Nehemiah the prophet dealt with this same situation with Israel just twenty years after the incident that was recorded in Ezra. Nehemiah even used King Solomon as an example of marrying outside of God's parameters. *"Did not Solomon, King of Israel, sin by these things? Yet among many nations there was no king like him, who was beloved of his God; and God made him King over all Israel. Nevertheless, pagan women caused even him to sin"* (Nehemiah 13:26).

Just like Solomon was loved by God, so are we. However, just because God loves us, that does not mean that He approves of us marrying who we will. We would never know it in today's society, but God has put certain stipulations and rules governing the desire for marriage. For example, the Scripture, *"Do not be unequally yoked together with unbelievers..."* *(2Corinthians 6:14a)* was given as a command, not a suggestion. These commands reflect God's great love for us by His not wanting our marriages to go off into shipwreck. And if it does, we may find divorce knocking on our door not to destroy us, but to save and rescue us from the mess we chose.

The rest of that verse says, *"For what fellowship has righteousness with lawlessness? And what communion has light with darkness"* *(2 Corinthians 6:14b)*. In other words, a Christian is to marry only a Christian. Moreover, a non-Christian is to only marry a non-Christian. Even though God commands us to marry within His family of the righteous, we can still be unequally yoked between different maturity levels or even with different personalities and interests.

STEERING YOU AWAY FROM GOD

God did not present the first man, Adam, with a hundred pretty ladies and say, "It's your choice, which one?" No, God made "one" pretty lady, and presented her to Adam and said, "she's for you" (See Genesis 2:22). Of course, Adam knew God only gives His best, and He said OK; and so it is with us. Not all marriages are approved by God; for it's *"...what GOD has joined together..."* *(Matthew 19:6b)*.

Even though God may bring a man and a woman together in a marriage relationship, that does not mean that one of the couples will not steer the other away from God, nor does it guarantee that their mate will continue to serve God at all. This happened with the first man, Adam, and his wife (See Genesis 3:4-13). You could not get a more perfect marriage than they had. This marriage was "made from heaven."

We must accept the fact that no matter how much we love a person, they still have their own will to do as they please. This fact is illustrated everyday concerning God and His lost family. *"For God so loved the world that He gave His only begotten Son, that whoever believes in Him should not perish but have everlasting life. [But when His Son] ...came to His own, ...HIS OWN DID NOT RECEIVE HIM" (John 3:16, 1:11).* How deeply that hurt our Lord Jesus. For He was *"...despised and rejected by [His own] men..." (Isaiah 53:3a).*

Our Lord Jesus does know the pain of what it's like to not have even His own family accept Him. And because He suffered the same thing with His family, He is able to strengthen our hearts to go on when we encounter similar situations (See Hebrews 2:18). Jesus said, *"Do not think that I came to bring peace on earth. I did not come to bring peace, BUT A SWORD. [For] He who loves ...[even family] ...more than me is not worthy of me" (Matthew 10:34-37).*

There will come a time when we shall give that account for what God told us to do. We will not give an account to God for our spouse, or for our friends, our brothers, sisters, or enemies, not anyone, but ourselves. For we shall be judged according to our own works, not why someone else caused us to disobey God's will (See Revelation 20:12b).

ABUSE

Abuse in its different manifestations is the most destructive tool that can be used by anyone against another person. It is designed to distort a person's view of reality and of God, thus keeping that person from having a fruitful life. When there is abuse going on in a relationship, it's time to separate. It doesn't matter how holy or good the person seems who is doing the violating.

There are different types of abuse and they are all designed for one thing and one thing only, DESTRUCTION! I believe all types of abuse can be put into one of these categories:

Physical Abuse: which is body torture that is used to subdue and control another person.

Sexual Abuse: torturing both a person physically and emotionally using unlawful sex acts as the weapon, i.e. prostitution, adultery, incest, homosexuality, rape, marriage rape, anything immoral or illegal sexually.

Verbal Abuse: designed to distort the truth a person holds about something or someone, including themselves in order to gain control over someone's mind.

Spiritual (religious) Abuse: used to manipulate another person to serve any other god than Jesus while many times exalting the abuser. At its worse, it's satanic ritual abuse, which many times include all the other categories of abuse.

Most sadly, all these types of abuses deeply scar the emotions of a person and usually greatly alters their perception and their ability to live life to its fullest. But there is hope. His name is Jesus. He has come to heal the broken-hearted.

If you have been abused and are hurt deeply inside, there is hope, healing, and full restoration. If you will yield your heart to the Holy Spirit sent from God to be our helper, He will lead you through every traumatic situation that you have been through into wholeness. The process is painful. However, on the other side of each "door of pain" is a place of joy, peace and rest.

The Holy Spirit works through the Word of God — the Bible. Which means, you must diligently give yourself to study of the Bible daily, surround yourself with godly people, turn your ears and eyes away from the secular media including TV, radio, movies, books and the like, and turn all of your heart over to

Jesus, He will tenderly minister life to you instead of death. Share the pain of your heart with Him while searching the Scriptures for the answers. As you're doing that, turn your eyes and ears to godly Christian books, tapes, videos, TV, radio stations and music that God can use to administer healing to your heart. You heard it said, "Eat the hay and leave the sticks?" There is a lot of christian stuff out there that has a lot of "sticks." Pick through them until you find a good hay mound. As you do these things you will gradually and continually become a whole, hurt-free, peaceful and joyful person. You will even start to like yourself. And how good that will feel!

VERBAL ABUSE

I am not going to discuss physical or sexual abuse because there are many good books written on the subject already. I'd rather expose the other two types of abuse that are rarely ever mentioned.

A person can be so verbally abused that they don't know what's true anymore. This abuse is designed to put a person in a numb state so they are unable to make clear, concise decisions. The path of verbal abuse leads a person from what they know as truth into a confused state. This confused state arises because the abuser consistently interjects lies as truth until the abused no longer knows what to believe. For example, we can see this happen when the abuser uses truths from the Bible to justify a lie, or the abuser twists the Bible's true intent to satisfy his own selfish motive. The sad part comes when the abused embraces the lies from the abuser as truth, thereby disregarding the real truth. At this point the abused feels like they are in chains of bondage with no way out. A trusted godly person is like a life preserver to the abused at this point. For *"the mouth of the righteous is a well of life" (Proverbs 10:11a)*.

There are three very important factors in verbal abuse. They are deception, confusion and reality or truth. We go through these steps during our lives until our belief system is built on a firm foundation of truth. The verbally abused spend most of their lives without a foundation of truth in their hearts and minds, but are in continual deception and confusion.

Confusion is a path — a means to reality (truth). Confusion is good ONLY when leaving deception and entering into reality (truth). When the Scripture says, *"...God is not the author of confusion..." (1Corinthians 14:33),* it is saying that **GOD DOES NOT GIVE *BOTH* TRUTH *AND* A LIE TO DECIDE FROM. HE IS *TRUTH!***

The three factors are:

Deception:
You think you understand, and believe you know the truth, when in fact you have embraced a lie as truth. Remember, **THE POWER OF DECEPTION IS THAT YOU DON'T KNOW YOU'RE DECEIVED.**

Confusion:
You have opened your heart to receive new understanding, which now conflicts with what you believed to be true. You're no longer sure. The "previously held" belief or knowledge may not be true in light of the new belief. **TWO OPPOSING THOUGHTS APPEARING TO BE TRUE IS CONFUSION.**

Reality (Truth):
We understand which is truly REAL and which is the counterfeit or false, then make the decision to embrace the truth; we leave confusion and enter into reality (truth). **TRUTH IS ALWAYS ABSOLUTE. IT DOES NOT CHANGE IN THE PRESENCE OF "NEW" TRUTH.**

If someone is "ignorant" instead of deceived, that is, they hold no knowledge or belief one way or another, they go from "ignorance to reality" without passing through any confusion. This is because the decision to choose between a lie and truth does not have to be made. A lie and truth are not always present at the same time to choose from.

The opposite often happens to people concerning their relationship with the true God. Instead of progressing from deception or being ignorant to truth, they digressed by exchanging the truth that they knew for a lie, and went back into deception — darkness. *"Because they knew God, they did not glorify Him as God, nor were thankful, but became futile in their thoughts, and their foolish hearts were darkened. WHO EXCHANGED THE TRUTH OF GOD FOR A LIE ...they did not like to retain God in their knowledge, [so] God gave them over to a debased mind, to do those things which are not fitting..." (Romans 1:21,25,28).* We must retain the truth of God in our hearts, which is the ONLY truth; otherwise we are dead while we live.

SPIRITUAL ABUSE

Let's consider spiritual abuse. When someone intentionally manipulates another person's perception of the only True God to suit his or her own purpose, it is spiritual abuse.

I'm not talking about when one spouse gives a half-hearted effort to serve the Lord and the other spouse gives the same half-hearted effort to prevent their mate from serving the Lord. In this case, they are not very serious about a personal relationship with God. I am talking about those who are continually attacked and abused: by physical means, verbal means or manipulation. This means those who had or earnestly desired a close relationship with the Lord but have been driven away because they've entangled themselves into a bad relationship or their relationship went bad after they were saved and their spouse or friend turned into "a wolf in sheep's clothing."

This type of abuse can manifest itself in many different ways. The more obvious manifestations are of the occult, such as satanic ritual abuse, or doing different types of witchcraft. Other manifestations are when one spouse pressures the other into joining a cult where others govern and control your life.

A cult is a religiously structured group of people that use all the right words of the Bible to attract others so they can control them. They use others to further their own cause. And they DO NOT have a personal relationship with Jesus Christ.

They are not "born-again." This is the dividing line between a cult and a true church of God.

The one extreme is when they want nothing to do with God or religion. The other extreme of spiritual abuse comes from a person who appears to be, or expresses himself to be, "very spiritual." They may not have a bad label on themselves, such as a satanist or witch. They may actually be accepted as a good person when in fact they are a wolf in sheep's clothing. Sometimes, the wolves actually believe they're sheep. Because they are deceived themselves, they propagate this same distortion of the reality of God upon their spouse and children. This abuse may eventually drive a person into confusion, or it may keep a person from personally knowing God altogether.

We feel like we are captives of our own heart at times because of contentious situations and unrest in our marriages. For *"...contentions are like the bars of a castle" (Proverbs 18:19).* We think of prisons that are made of brick and steel as the only places where people are held in captivity. Not so! Many people are held captive in their own homes by their own spouse. These bricks and steel bars are in their heart.

If your home is a prison because of physical, sexual, spiritual or heart-destroying verbal abuse, whether to you or your children, it is highly recommended that you immediately leave that environment if you desire to ever be healed and made whole. You must confide in a trusted friend, find some place to stay, seek out a church that understands and is willing to help, and go to the authorities and file the proper complaints. (To get you started, we placed a *Sources of Help* section in the rear of this book or you may visit our website: www.DivorceHope.com for updates.) *"For there is no authority except from God, and the authorities that exist are appointed by God. FOR RULERS ARE NOT A TERROR TO GOOD WORKS, BUT TO EVIL" (Romans 13:1b,3a).*

It is very important to go and stay with a trusted friend. It is not recommended to return to a potentially abusive environment. Your very life is at stake, physically and spiritually. Then you can pray and get before God and find out what to do next. Normally, it takes several years for an abusive person to clean up their act with proper counseling and therapy.

(See SOURCES in back of book.) I want to emphasize this: **DIVORCE IS NOT SIN IN ITSELF. DIVORCE IS A MEANS TO "PRESERVE" ONE PERSON FROM THE CORRUPTION OF ANOTHER** (See Ezra 9:1-10:4).

GOD HAS NO "MISTAKES"

Some may feel like you were a "mistake" in life (whether it was by a conception that was not wanted, neglect, rape, incest, having been a "throw-away child" or whatever) but you aren't. The Lord spoke to my heart one day and said, *"I did not predestinate you from a perfect order, BUT FROM AN ORDER THAT WAS OUT OF ORDER."* Meaning, God did not plan the future from a point of everyone being perfect. Instead, He looked into the future and saw all the "mistakes" of life, weighed the attitudes and motives of people's hearts and said, "It was not their fault. Therefore, THESE are the ones that I have chosen." Isn't that grand?

For we have been *"...predestinated [from an order that was out of order] according to the purpose of Him who works all things according to the counsel of His will... For you see ...that not many mighty, not many noble, are called. BUT GOD HAS CHOSEN THE FOOLISH THINGS [THAT'S US] OF THE WORLD TO PUT TO SHAME THE WISE, AND GOD HAS CHOSEN THE WEAK THINGS of the world to put to shame the things that are mighty; AND THE BASE THINGS [THOSE WHO THINK THEY'RE THE LOWEST] OF THE WORLD AND THE THINGS WHICH ARE DESPISED GOD HAS CHOSEN"* (Ephesians 1:11, 1Corinthians 1:26-28).

Often, when someone is a victim of someone else's selfish choice, they feel they're a lost part of God's "perfect order." But it's the order that's "out of order" that God has chosen. Be encouraged! God Himself has chosen you. And what a wonderful God He is!

TWO TYPES OF PEACE

There are two types of "peace." One type of peace is between "God and man" (See Luke 2:13,14) and the other type of peace is between "man and man" (See Matthew 10:32-34, John 14:27). This word peace means "to join," or "to set at one, again."[7]

The peace between man and man is the *"...peace the world gives..." (John 14:27)*. The peace between God and man is from God himself. Jesus gave us His peace so we can be joined to Him. *"Peace I leave with you, MY PEACE I give to you; not as the world gives do I give to you" (John 14:27)*. Whenever there is peace between two parties, it causes a joining. Whenever there is strife (enmity) between two parties, it causes a separation. Because peace brings unity, there is a constant battle raging for our soul. The world is battling for us to be joined to its ways, while God is battling for us to be joined to Him. And whomever we chose to join, we by default become separated from the other. The daily question of our lives is, "Will we be at peace with God or the world?"

When it was time for Jesus to come and to be born in the earth, the angels praised God, saying *"Glory to God in the highest, and on earth PEACE, good will TOWARD MEN!" (Luke 2:14)*. Notice this peace was from God, "toward men," not "between" man and man. The way for God and man to "be at one again" had arrived: Jesus, the Son of God Himself (See Romans 5:1).

THE NATURE OF PEACE

Many relationships today do not have peace, mainly because we don't understand what peace is, whom it's from, whom it's for, and what its purpose is. The true understanding of the peace of God is found in the book of Hebrews. Pay particular attention to the word "chastening," and how it's used.

"If you endure chastening, God deals with you as with sons; for what son is there whom a father does not chasten? But if you are without chastening, of which all have become partakers, then you are illegitimate and not sons. Furthermore, we have had human fathers who corrected us, and we paid them respect. Shall we not much more readily be in subjection to the Father of spirits and live? For they indeed for a few days chastened us as seemed best to them, BUT HE FOR OUR PROFIT, THAT WE MAY BE PARTAKERS OF HIS HOLINESS. Now no CHASTENING seems to be joyful for the present, but painful; nevertheless, afterward it YIELDS the PEACEABLE FRUIT of righteousness to those who have been trained by it" (Hebrews 12:7-11).*

Notice that "chastening" is a SEED of "peace." Otherwise, how could it "yield" the "peaceable fruit" of righteousness? Everything produces after it's own kind (See Genesis 1:11). You must have a "peace" tree to produce "peaceable fruit." And you must have "peace" seeds to grow a "peace" tree. Therefore chastening, which is receiving correction in our lives, is the "seed" of peace. Going through the process of correcting a situation in our life is not always peaceful, but AFTERWARDS, it leads to peace.

We all want peace in our families. But we have misunderstood not WHAT peace is, but rather, WHO peace is and what He's like. *"For HE HIMSELF [Jesus] IS OUR PEACE, WHO HAS MADE BOTH ONE, and has broken down the middle wall of separation"* (Ephesians 2:14). To understand God's peace, we must keep in mind its definition and more importantly, its nature: which is "to join, or set at one again." It's incredible to think of peace as something or someone that has an aggressive nature, even to the point of causing the "walls" in our lives that are separating Him from us to be "broken down," especially if these walls are relationships.

The reason for this aggressive nature of God's peace is to preserve. God's peace will do whatever it takes to join us back to Him, but only if we yield. The peace of God is released in us through our relationship with Him. His peace causes a separation in our lives of what is, and what is not of God. *"Now may the God of peace Himself SANCTIFY [SEPARATE] YOU COMPLETELY; and may your whole spirit, soul, and body BE*

71

PRESERVED BLAMELESS at the coming of our Lord Jesus Christ"
(1Thessalonians 5:23). "And [ultimately] the God of peace will
crush satan under your feet shortly" (Romans 16:20). The peace
of God works in every area of our life to bring us to God.

THE SEPARATING POWER OF PEACE

The old cliché "Don't rock the boat" is used many times to
describe "peace." Even when there is a mutual agreement not to
make waves, it is not true peace. True peace always carries with
it a separating unto that which is holy, pure or true. When God's
peace comes into a situation where the righteous and
unrighteous mix, there will be separating, chastisement or war
(See 1Corinthians 7:15, Hebrews 12:7-11, Romans 16:20.)

If we do not have peace in our families or homes, it is
because we have not allowed peace to "rule" the affairs of our
lives (See Colossians 3:15). Peace will lead us out of wrong
situations. It will separate us unto the Lord Himself. Most of the
time, this process is not what we would call "peaceful." In fact,
sometimes it can become very violent (See Romans 16:20,
Colossians 1:20). Most of the time the peace of God upsets the
proverbial "apple cart" of our lives. This explains why husbands
and wives, and those in close relationships have such a difficult
time making decisions that "appear" to cause separation. Hence,
**THE PATH TO TRUE PEACE IS ALWAYS UNITY *AFTER*
SEPARATION!**

To illustrate the meaning of peace "to be set at one,
again" in another way, I'm going to speak of two classes of
people: the Christian and the non-Christian, those who know
and those who do not know the Lord Jesus in a personal way. In
fact, God recognizes only two types of people in the world: those
who know Him and those who need to.

We tend to socialize with those people who are like us, or
those we want to be like. Hence, "birds of a feather do flock
together." That is, we socialize with those who have the same
heart motivations, the same attitudes, the same hurts and
dysfunctions, the same talents and gifts. This explains why even

Christians tend to embrace that which is unlike God. It's an inward hurt, an unsanctified area of the heart that wants to reunite with its like nature, and be at peace. Because of this, there is a continual battle raging. Before coming to God, we were all part of this fallen world. We didn't know God personally. We only knew about Him. Because we have been born again and not part of this fallen sinful world, the peace "of the world" is continually pulling us back to itself through the influence of the parts of our heart that have not yet been changed by the power of God. This is called "the old nature" (See John 14:27). This is why there are battles going on in our hearts. Thus, the peace of the world is trying to unify itself at the same time as the peace of God.

Therefore, **TO BE AT PEACE, YOU MUST WAR TO SEPARATE.** We can see this as *"the flesh lusts [puts hard pressure] against the Spirit, and the Spirit [puts hard pressure] against the flesh" (Galatians 5:17).* This is why sin feels good for a season (See Hebrews 11:25). It's because of the peace it brings when it unites with the sinful area of our heart. We can now understand why many people stay in the "comfort zone;" the carnal nature is at peace with those activities. To get to where we are led by the Spirit of God, the peace of God will separate our lives from the carnal ways we live, hence tipping our world up-side down. Nevertheless, by the grace of God, we will ultimately be at peace with God and not the world.

Peace and marriage go hand-in-hand. We can't have a true marriage without peace (See 1Corinthians 7:15), nor can we have a relationship with God without peace between Him and us (See Ephesians 2:14-18). If we want to be at peace with God and have peace in our family, we must make those tough decisions to allow peace to rule. The Lord never said it was going to be easy, but it will be much better.

4

WHO JOINED YOU TOGETHER?

DID GOD JOIN US TOGETHER?

"Therefore, what GOD *has joined..." (Matthew 19:6b).*

It is commonly believed that every marriage between a man and a woman is "joined" by God and God's blessings are on the marriage. We see from the Scriptures of Ezra, chapter 9 and 10, and Nehemiah, chapter 13 that this is just not true. Let me take this to an extreme to more clearly reveal this truth.

Would God come to a wedding of a man and a woman who are professing active worshipers of satan? Would God "witness" this marriage and pronounce His blessing on them when this couple actively serves another god and renounces the God of all creation? Do you think God would have a close intimate relationship with the devil and at the same time command us to *"...have NO fellowship with the unfruitful works of darkness, but ...[tells us to] ...expose them..." (Ephesians 5:11).* Whatever God commands us to do, He Himself does.

Another type of marriage that God has no part of is a homosexual marriage. For *"you shall not lie with a male as with a woman. IT IS AN ABOMINATION" (Leviticus 18:22). "Therefore, God also gave them up to uncleanness, in the lusts of their hearts, to dishonor their bodies among themselves ...for even their women exchanged the natural use for what is against nature. Likewise, also the men, leaving the natural use of the woman, burned in their lust for one another, men with men committing what is shameful ...and they did not like to retain God in their knowledge..." (Romans 1:24,26-28).* Do you think God actually joins these people in a holy marriage when He Himself condemns the marriage itself?

GOD DOES NOT JOIN TOGETHER WHAT HE DOES NOT APPROVE OF! However, He does allow a marriage to continue when one spouse gets saved provided that the spouse who is now His child is able to pursue a godly lifestyle with his or her children. In this case, the entire family is blessed; otherwise, divorce is in order.

The Scripture that commands us not to pull apart "what God has put together" deals with "what GOD has put together!"

If God did not put the marriage together, we shouldn't be in it in the first place. If we are in such a marriage, we can get out.

Each bad marriage has a different set of circumstances. Therefore, the guidelines are: you and your children must be safe and have a good environment at home; you must be able to fully pursue a devoted lifestyle to God. If this is the case, God will sanctify the marriage and the family because of the holy life of the godly spouse (See 1Corinthians 7:12-16).

DID WE JOIN OURSELVES TOGETHER?

If God did not join us together, then WE must have joined ourselves together. And if we chose to join ourselves together, we are not in a position to receive the same blessings on our marriage that God gives to a couple He has joined together.

God's people who have *"...married the daughter [or son] of a foreign god ...[they] cover the alter of the Lord with tears, with weeping and crying; so He [GOD] DOES NOT REGARD THE OFFERING [OF OUR PRAYERS] ANYMORE, NOR RECEIVE IT WITH GOODWILL FROM YOUR HANDS. Yet you say, 'For what reason?'" (Malachi 2:11b, 13,14a).* When there is a marriage or divorce that God does not approve of, we can be assured that God will not pronounce His blessing upon it, or answer our prayers, unless we repent and make right the situation that we did outside of His will.

Since *"...there is NO authority except from God, and the authorities that exist are appointed by God" (Romans 13:1b)*, **ONE CAN BE "JOINED TOGETHER" BY THE EXECUTORS OF GOD'S LAW *WITHOUT* RECEIVING THE BLESSINGS OF THE LAWGIVER HIMSELF.**

If God does not "witness" a marriage, if it is not approved by Him, it doesn't matter who we have to perform the wedding. It could be a justice of the peace, a judge, pastor, priest or whoever. If God does not approve it, it's not approved! The state's governing laws pertaining to age, citizenship, family relationship, or sex may approve the marriage. But these laws only govern a man from the outside. The Bible, God's Word, governs a man from the inside, because it *"...is living and powerful, and sharper than any two-edged sword, piercing even to the division of soul [where a couple is joined together] and spirit, and of joints and marrow, and is a discerner of the thoughts and intents of the heart"* (Hebrews 4:12).

IF WE WANT OUR MARRIAGE TO BE BLESSED BY GOD, GOD MUST APPROVE OF OUR MARRIAGE, otherwise, we will receive the very minimum amount of blessings from God, if any. If we do not repent but continue in our stubbornness, we *"are treasuring up for ...[ourselves] ...wrath ..."(Romans 2:5).* Then we wonder why God allowed this to happen? How did we get into this terrible relationship anyway? We blame everybody but ourselves.

BECAUSE OF PEER PRESSURE

Society today puts great pressure on us to have a sexual relationship with another person outside of marriage. The prime thrust of this pressure comes through those with whom we associate and the general media. Television, radio, movies, and the printed page, such as books and magazines promote humanistic and evolutionistic teachings. When we have acted out and succumbed to those pressures, we know that a part of us has been *"...conformed to this world..."* (Romans 12:2). We have taken on the form of the mold of what the world wants us to be instead of what God wants us to be.

Building a daily intimate relationship with Jesus can reverse this process; think upon and do what He says in the Bible. By having an intimate relationship with God, we will gravitate toward associating with those of His people who walk upright before Him. This, of course, further strengthens our relationship with Him. The peers that we once associated with are no longer a major part of our life. Now, we have new peers. Instead of these peers pressuring us to go into immorality, we are influenced toward morality and doing right. It takes work and a determined effort to walk upright before God. It's not an easy road, but it's the fulfillment of life itself.

OK, let's say we didn't quite walk uprightly before God for whatever the reason. It's not the end of the world. As we repent, *"He is faithful and just to forgive us our sins and to cleanse us from all unrighteousness" (1John 1:9).* With that, we can start over again. But what if the sexual experience was a beginning of a pregnancy, a baby?

GOD'S WILL FOR MARRIAGE IS NOT BASED ON HAVING A BABY

Being pregnant and having a baby outside of wedlock does not dictate God's will for marriage. People have gotten married for this very reason. Nearly all of those who have married did so because they were taught by the religious system or by their parents that they HAD to marry the father of the child. Some women were raped; other women were reaching out to a male for the affection they never received from their own fathers. Sadly, they discovered that along with the affection they found, came the requirement for them to have sex. Some women found themselves pregnant and their life of sex was exposed. It didn't matter if they had sex with one or many; you HAD to marry the male who supposedly got you pregnant.

Forcing a pregnant woman to marry may be very commendable for the unborn child, but it's not totally God's heart. Even though God desires for every child to have a father, He gave that discretion to the father of the family. For *"if a man seduces a virgin not betrothed [engaged] and lies with her, he shall surely pay a dowry for her to become his wife. [BUT] IF HER FATHER UTTERLY REFUSES TO GIVE HER TO HIM, he shall [still] pay money equivalent to the dowry of virgins" (Exodus 22:16, 17 AMP).* The *reason* for the dowry is similar to today's "support payments" awarded by the court to the woman. Notice that God did not take into consideration at all the fact that the woman got pregnant. **THE CONSIDERATION FOR MARRIAGE WAS BASED UPON THE FORNICATION, NOT ON GETTING PREGNANT FROM THE SEXUAL ACTS. THE DISCRETION IS LEFT UP TO THE FATHER OF THE WOMAN, EVEN IF SHE IS PREGNANT.** God knows that every situation is different.

Because of the authority given to the father to allow his daughter to marry or not to marry, the consequences or blessings rest upon the daughter. Some fathers have made wise choices in allowing their daughters to marry, and some have not. Marrying a person primarily because a baby is involved can remove one further from God's will and may actually be "jumping from the frying pan into the fire." Two wrongs do not make a right.

Unsanctified Marriages

We tend to think that EVERY marriage is blessed and seen as holy by God because of what we've been taught, but not every marriage is! God does not call holy that which is unholy. God desires us to be like Himself, to be able to *"...distinguish between holy and unholy, and between unclean and clean"* (Leviticus 10:10). If we do not have this discernment, we can make or continue in a fatal marriage. **JUST BECAUSE WE ARE MARRIED BY THE LAW, IT DOESN'T MEAN THAT THE LAWGIVER HIMSELF HAS MARRIED US.**

Many people stay trapped for years in marriages that God will not bless. Many are abused slaves to their spouse. They cry out, "Why doesn't God bless our marriage?" Blessings are given to the person who will call upon Him, love Him, and put Him first. God does bless us as much as He can, but many times it falls far short of what we really need because we block God.

Some unsanctified marriages may have a partner who is a homosexual or lesbian. Some husbands even rape their wives. Other marriage partners may be having sex with animals. Others may be very abusive or having sexual pleasures with their children or someone else's children. Some marriages have deteriorated over time, while others may have been bad from the start. Some unsanctified marriages may not have any outward manifestations of uncleanness at first. Some of the more common things that cause a marriage partner to be unclean are alcoholism, drugs, lustful sex, or a party spirit. The Bible has much to say about being a part of these things. Examples in the

Bible are found in Ephesians 5:3-12, 1Corinthians 6:9-11, and 1Corinthians 5:1-13.

People live and die without ever experiencing the blessings that God pronounces on a sanctified marriage. They feel trapped and so continue in abusive situations because of what they have been taught (or not taught). For example, you may have been taught that once you've been married you can never get a divorce because "God hates divorce," no matter how wrong, abusive, or unholy the marriage is. The truth is, God is more for the divorce than He is for the marriage. However, He is able to change a heart to stop the unclean and unrighteous acts if that person will call out and yield their life totally to Him.

In most bad marriages, it is not easy to make wise decisions because of the complexity of issues, the children that are involved, and a myriad of other situations that arise. However, if we will go to God with an open heart and tell Him that we're willing to follow Him no matter what, even to the point of dissolving a marriage, He will start working in our life. This can be very painful. You may want to quit many times as God takes you through the process. The situation will appear impossible, and truly, it is. *"The things which are impossible with man ARE POSSIBLE with God" (Luke 18:27).* God never did call us to do the impossible in our own strength and ability. First we must become weak in our own ability. Then when we cry out in our weakness, GOD'S *"...strength is made perfect in [our] weakness. For when I am weak, THEN I am strong" (2Corinthians 12:9a,10b).*

If you are in this kind of situation and need God's help, pray:

Dear Jesus, you know my situation. I've really messed up. Your Word says that if I confess my sins before you, you are faithful and just to forgive me and to clean me up and enable me to make a new start in life by living for you. I confess my sins to you, Lord, and I ask you to forgive me. Jesus, I surrender my life to you fully. I want to live for you alone. I ask you to start creating whatever circumstances are necessary to get my life into the flow of your perfect will. I thank you, in Jesus' name. Amen.

5

WHO IS DOING THE SEPARATING?

WHO IS THE MAN?

"Is it lawful for a MAN *to divorce..." (Matthew 19:3).*

"Therefore what God has joined together, let not MAN *separate"* *(Matthew 19:6b).*

Who is this "man?" Who is the one promoting the separation? Can anybody outside the marriage divorce the husband and wife if they themselves did not want to be divorced? Of course not! You may be able to physically separate the husband and wife from each other, but not the marriage or "oneness" that they possess in their hearts. The "man" in Matthew 19:3b, 6b are the marriage partners. *"Therefore what God has joined together, let not ...[the marriage partners] ...separate" (Matthew 19:6b).* The Scripture is saying concerning a God-ordained marriage, that the husband and wife are not to allow selfish motives to rule their hearts thus causing a separation or divorce. When a marriage covenant has been badly violated, we can ask for our heavenly Father's help to dissolve it. The Scripture does NOT say, "therefore what God has joined together, let not GOD separate," but "let not man (the marriage partners) separate" out of self-gratification.

There is a vast difference between us doing something from our own self-gratification, and us carrying out a needed action to save our family. The very actions themselves that we carry out may appear to "look" the same, but the unseen part that makes the difference between a sinful act and a righteous act, is the desire of your heart. **DIVORCE ITSELF IS NOT WRONG, BUT WHEN IT'S USED FOR SELFISH PLEASURE, IT IS!**

TO WHICH DIVORCE DID GOD SAY, "I HATE DIVORCE?"

We have heard this Scripture: *"the Lord God of Israel says that HE HATES DIVORCE" (Malachi 2:16).* This is almost always quoted as if God hates all divorces in general. But that's just not true. We have previously read from the Bible books of Ezra,

Nehemiah, Jeremiah, Deuteronomy and 1Corinthians that God is not against divorce. Then why all the confusion concerning why God said that "He hates divorce?" The reason for the confusion is because there are TWO "kinds" of marriages and TWO "divorces" being mentioned in the Malachi 2:11-16 passage.

The "divorces" were not official divorces; they didn't need to be. They were already previously married and "unofficially" married again. The Hebrew word *shalach*[18] means "putting away"— a separation, as correctly translated in most Bibles. However, the King James and a number of newer versions have incorrectly translated *shalach* as to mean: divorce. It never meant divorce and it doesn't mean divorce. The word was most likely translated as "divorce" to fit what was taught in the church. *Shalach* is just a common word used throughout the Old Testament which means to: go, separate or to send. That's it!

So why did God angrily say that He *"...hated putting away [a separation]?" "...Because you have not kept My ways [concerning marriage, divorce and remarriage] but have SHOWN PARTIALITY IN THE LAW"* (Malachi 2:9). The Law specifically stated that when a man got a divorce from his wife that he was to write *"...her a CERTIFICATE OF DIVORCE, put it in her hand, AND [shalach] send her out [put her away]..."* (Deuteronomy 24:1). God also commanded them not to marry anyone who did not serve him — who served a foreign god (See Nehemiah 13:25-30).

Instead, men separated from their wives without ever giving them a Certificate of Divorce and then illegally married someone else. This is why the Lord said that they were still "their wife by covenant." The marriage covenant had never been dissolved by the Divorce Certificate.

"The Lord's holy institution which He loves...the Lord has been witness between you and the wife of your youth...[and] SHE [STILL] IS YOUR COMPANION AND YOUR WIFE BY COVENANT. For the Lord God of Israel says that He hates divorce [shalach], [separating without a Certificate of Divorce].... He has [illegally] married the daughter of a foreign god. May the Lord cut off ...the

man who does this being awake and aware" (Malachi 2:11,12a,14b,c,16a).

Because these men had remarried illegally — separated from their wives without giving them a Certificate of Divorce, they were in adultery as Jesus stated: *"Furthermore it has been said, "Whoever PUTS AWAY [separates from {apoluo}] his wife, LET HIM GIVE HER A CERTIFICATE OF DIVORCE. But I say to you that whoever PUTS AWAY [separates and remarries without being divorced from] his wife for any reason except sexual immorality causes her to commit adultery: and whoever marries a woman who is PUT AWAY [separated without being divorced {apoluo}] commits adultery" (Matthew 5:31-32).* (The Lord never forgot about the Malachi incident when He came to earth to redeem lost man.)

The Old Testament Hebrew word *shalach* and the New Testament Greek word *apoluo* are equivalent which will be discussed later.

Because these disobedient men still had "un-divorced" wives, the Lord did not command them to give their illegal wives a Certificate of Divorce, rather, they simply had to "separate, put them away, *[shalach]*." **SO DID GOD HATE DIVORCE? *NO!* RATHER, GOD HATED THAT THE HUSBANDS WERE SEPARATING FROM THEIR WIVES WITHOUT GIVING THEM A CERTIFICATE OF DIVORCE WHICH WOULD ENABLE THEM TO GET REMARRIED. *THIS* IS WHAT GOD HATES!**

The men of Israel were SEPARATING from their wives for self-gratifying reasons. God Himself was a "witness" at their original marriage ceremony which was still in effect. The marriage covenant was never dissolved by a Certificate of Divorce. The men remarried outside their own culture (race) and tribe. God considered the children they bore unholy because of the mixed marriages bringing curses into their families (See Ezra 9:1,2, Nehemiah 13:26-30).

Because of these unauthorized marriages, the Word of God came to Ezra and Nehemiah to have the men and women of Israel who had done this thing, to separate from their spouse and even from their children (See Ezra 9:1, 11-12, 10:3, Nehemiah 13:23-27). In this situation, God's command was to "put them away, separate yourselves from them!" This was NOT the kind of marriage to which God was saying, "I hate divorce!" He was saying loudly, "Get out of these wrong marriages!"

DIVORCE IS A METHOD TO SEPARATE THE ONE, AND MAKE THEM INTO TWO just as a surgeon's knife is used to separate the cancerous flesh from the healthy flesh. Both operations are good. Divorce can be used to kill a righteous marriage, just as a surgeon's knife can be used to kill a healthy person.

GOD BRINGS TOGETHER AND GOD PULLS APART

We act as though we believe that once God has "joined together" a man and a woman, that He somehow loses His sovereign position as God, and cannot separate the two if the situation warrants it. As we have just read from Ezra and Nehemiah, that is just not so. God is God! For *"...He has mercy on whom He wills, and whom He wills He hardens"* (Romans 9:18). (See also Exodus 33:19.)

We see God using His sovereign right to remove the crown, a type of family headship, from one of the greatest kings ever: Solomon. *"[For] ...King Solomon loved many foreign women ...[For] ...the Lord had said to the children of Israel, 'YOU SHALL NOT INTERMARRY WITH THEM, NOR THEY WITH YOU. Surely they will turn away your hearts after their gods...' So the Lord became angry with Solomon because his heart had turned from the Lord God of Israel. Therefore the Lord said to Solomon, 'BECAUSE YOU HAVE DONE THIS [married against My will], and have not kept My covenant and My statutes, which I have commanded you, I WILL SURELY TEAR THE KINGDOM AWAY FROM YOU and give it to your servant'"* (1Kings 11:1,2,9,11).

It has been wrongly taught that breaking a marriage covenant should NEVER be done. But we forget that God is jealous for a righteous holy-living people. When we join into a covenant agreement that flies right in the face of His will, be assured that He will expect us to correct it; not just to keep on going as if nothing had happened and ask Him to "bless" it.

The vow, "to death do us part" that we make at our wedding is not found in the Bible. We can't even keep ourselves by our OWN strength in the love of God, and yet we are going to commit ourselves to love someone else forever? A scriptural vow that would be more appropriate to promise one another on our wedding day would be: "By the GRACE OF GOD, AND THROUGH HIS STRENGTH, I GIVE myself to you all the days of my life, to have and to hold, to love and to cherish...." For in ourselves we are weak. However, because of being born again into Christ, we CAN do all things through Christ who gives us the strength through His grace (See Philippians 4:13). As we yield our heart to God, everyday His glorious love will flow from Him, through us, and to our mate. The only thing that will ever separate our hearts on this earth is when we pass on to meet our Maker.

The Scripture, *Exodus 20:3,* says for us to *"have no other gods before [us]"* deals with relationship. For RELATIONSHIP IS COVENANT! Therefore, if there is a relationship in our life that we want more than what the Lord God wants us to have, we are in covenant relationship outside of His will. When God's relationship with us is interfered with by another relationship, He will ask us to make the proper adjustments in our heart or break the relationship. If we won't give the relationship its proper place or separate on our own, He Himself will start the process for it to break. The very bonds of the relationship will start to crumble and many times, it isn't pleasant.

That's what happened to King Solomon; *"...because you have done this [you entered a marriage covenant you weren't supposed to], and have not kept MY covenant ...I will surely tear the kingdom away from you..." (1Kings 11:11).* God, in revealing the steadfastness of His heart, used King Solomon as an example to the future generations.

A NATION: A REFLECTION OF MARRIAGES

Why does God command us not to marry outside of His family, and specifically, for us to ask Him to choose our mate for us? What is behind satan's strategy in hurrying us to marry without first seeking God and waiting for the mate that He is so delightfully preparing for us?

God is the one who created the earth and the fullness thereof. The whole world and all of creation was given to the first man, Adam to rule over. Adam gave it over to satan and now both righteousness and evil cohabitate in the same world (See Luke 4:6, Proverbs 18:21). Because of this there must be a separation between the two natures. Therefore, we must choose between the nature of "Life," and the nature of "Death" (See Deuteronomy 30:19).

Satan's strategy for the husband or wife is to have an unrighteous spouse, thereby mixing the godly with the ungodly and producing unrighteous children. Because the children are our future leaders, they will lead the people away from God and from doing right. *"For righteous exalts a nation, but sin is a reproach to any people" (Proverbs 14:34).* Moreover, when a fair portion of that generation of children lives out their corruption and unrighteous, the future of the nation is in jeopardy. Therefore in this case, separation and divorce is a method to save.

When the desire to marry comes from our own selfish heart, for our own selfish purpose, and for our own selfish gratification, you can be assured that disaster is looming in the air. *"Did not Solomon, King of Israel, sin by these things? Yet among many nations there was no king like him, who was beloved of his God; and God made him King over all Israel. Nevertheless, pagan women caused even him to sin" (Nehemiah 13:26).* This caused Solomon's whole nation to crumble, because families make up a nation.

Therefore, when separating or divorce comes from God's heart through man, it's to save people. That is whether the marriage went bad, or was bad from the beginning. God is doing the separating to have a righteous people, for *"righteousness exalts a nation, but sin is a reproach to any people."*

WHEN MAN SEPARATES, IT CAN BE TEMPORARY

Divorce or separation can be either temporary or permanent, depending on who the initiator is. If it's man, the divorce or separation can be temporary, but when it's God, the divorce is permanent.

First, let's look at the initiator being man. This is when the desire for a divorce flows out of a spouse's own selfish heart, not from God's heart to the spouse.

Suppose a marriage partner initiates a divorce (not a separation):

The Bible says, *"When a man takes a wife and marries her, and it happens that ...he has found some uncleanness in her, and HE WRITES her a certificate of divorce ...sends her out of his house ...and goes and BECOMES ANOTHER MAN'S WIFE, if the latter husband dies who took her as his wife, THEN her former husband who divorced her MUST NOT TAKE HER BACK to be his wife..."* (Deuteronomy 24:1-4). When WE have divorced our spouse from our own selfish heart, we can take them back — remarry them, if they have not already remarried. However, if they have already married someone else and their spouse divorced them or died, we are not allowed to marry them again. And if we do, it's an abomination to God, for it brings sin on our home and country (See Deuteronomy 24:4).

Now let's look at one of the marriage partners initiating a separation (not a divorce):

"...A wife is not to DEPART from her husband. But even if she does depart, let her remain unmarried OR BE RECONCILED TO HER HUSBAND. And a husband is not to divorce his wife" (1Corinthians 7:10-11).

This Scripture is NOT referring to a finalized legal divorce, but a "separation" only. The Greek word used for "depart" is *chorizo*, and it means "to place room between, to separate."[8] This is clearly seen because the husband and wife before the separation are STILL husband and wife AFTER the separation. For the wife is to *"...be reconciled to HER HUSBAND"* (1 Corinthians 7:11a), not, *"...HER FORMER HUSBAND who divorced her..." (Deuteronomy 24:4a)*. If she were divorced, she wouldn't have a husband. But when you're just separated, you still have a husband.

Using the husband and wife example in this Scripture, let me explain what is happening, and what regularly happens in relationships.

The wife says to the husband, "I'm leaving you!" That statement immediately starts the husband to pursue after his wife who is leaving. "Oh, no, you're not," he says. This constant chasing may go on for some time. But after awhile the husband gives up the pursuit, then the wife starts to draw back to her husband. As long as the husband seems to go away from his wife, or not to display to her a pursuing heart, she will return in many cases. *"...A wife is not to depart [separate] from her husband. But even if she does depart [separate] let her remain unmarried or BE RECONCILED TO HER HUSBAND. And a husband is not to [spitefully] DIVORCE HIS WIFE " (1Corinthians 7:10-11)*.

At this point the wife returns and they both come to an agreement to reconcile. However, because now the wife is pursuing the husband, the husband's heart somehow feels justified to let his wife feel some pain. So he says, "forget the reconciliation, I want a divorce!" And so is the case in the above Scripture. If your spouse is willing to have a godly reconciliation, don't divorce them.

There is one last thing in this Scripture I would like to point out that's very important. It says, *"A wife is not to depart from her husband. But even if she does depart, let her REMAIN UNMARRIED..." (1Corinthians 7:11a)*. The Greek work translated "unmarried" is *agamos*.[9] It's the negative form of *gamos*,[10] which means, "no nuptials" — no relationship of or having to do with mating. To remain "unmarried" DOES NOT mean you cannot get remarried, but you should not have a "marriage relationship" (sex) with anyone else, but to be *"...reconciled to your husband [or wife]" (1Corinthians 7:11a)*. When a separation occurs, we're to be abstinent. Sexual relations dictate union in God's eyes. When the husband and wife are joined together in sex, *"...the two shall become ONE FLESH" (Matthew 19:5)*.

WHEN GOD DIVORCES, IT'S PERMANENT

When it's God's desire for us to divorce our spouse, it's done permanently. When God pulls apart there is no going back. It's over. He dissolves that union forever. Let's look at the story of King Saul, for example. I want you to notice two things about this situation. First, God anointed Saul and made him king over Israel. Then because of disobedience, God removed the anointing and rejected Saul from being king.

The Lord told Samuel (the prophet) that He had chosen Saul to be King over the nation of Israel to deliver them from out of the oppression of the Philistines. Therefore, the Lord had Samuel anoint Saul and pronounce Him as king (See 1Samuel 9:15-10:11). And it came to pass that the Word of Lord came to King Saul through Samuel, the prophet, because of what Amalek did to Israel. *"Thus says the Lord of hosts, 'I will punish what Amalek did to Israel, how he ambushed him on the way when he came up from Egypt. Now go and attack Amalek, and utterly destroy ALL that they have, and do not spare them'" (1Samuel 15:2,3)*. King Saul did not do as the Lord commanded, but *"SPARED the best of the sheep and the oxen" (1Samuel 15:15)*.

It doesn't matter how great we are or what position we hold, it grieves God when we defiantly disobey Him. Sometimes it appears we do well when we save what looks like the best when in fact, the portion we saved will actually be our downfall. For the Lord said, *"I greatly regret that I have set up Saul as King..." (1Samuel 15:10)*.

We may think we are the only ones who hurt inside when a decision to separate has to be made. It hurt God greatly to separate Saul from the kingship. Then Samuel said to Saul by the Spirit of the Lord, *"...because you have rejected the Word of the Lord, He also has rejected you from being King"* *(1Samuel 15:23b)*. Saul was cut to the heart and said, "I have sinned" and asked forgiveness for his disobedience (See 1 Samuel 15:24,25). Even though Saul repented, God separated him from that position. God knew it was the end because Saul would never accomplish God's mission the way God wanted it carried out. Then Samuel said, *"The Lord has torn the kingdom of Israel from you today and has given it to a neighbor of yours, who is better than you"* *(1Samuel 15:28)*.

Samuel was very hurt and he "mourned for Saul." *"[Then] ...the Lord said to Samuel, 'How long will you mourn for Saul, seeing I have rejected him...'"* *(1Samuel 16:1)*. Even though Samuel mourned for Saul, *"Samuel went no more to see Saul until the day of his death [For] the Spirit of the Lord DEPARTED... from Saul..."* *(1Samuel 15:35,16:14)*.

This is sad in a way, but we must turn our backs on the past and the "could have's," and keep our eyes on the One who will never leave us, nor forsake us, even until the end of the age. It doesn't seem fair that God would permanently separate, but it is, *"FOR THE LORD DOES NOT SEE AS MAN SEES; FOR MAN LOOKS AT THE OUTWARD APPEARANCE, BUT THE LORD LOOKS AT THE HEART"* *(1Samuel 16:7)*. The Lord knows that if we don't separate when He calls us to separate, we will never make it with Him. We will become, a "could have." *"For MANY are called, but FEW are chosen"* *(Matthew 22:14)*.

Consider King Solomon who was greatly beloved of God. He married women whom the Lord commanded him not to; consequently, they turned his heart away from God. God then tore the kingdom away from Him.

Another tragic story is about Moses and the people of Israel. Moses talked with God "face to face," while the people of Israel "walked contrary" to the Lord (See Deuteronomy 5:4, Leviticus 26:40). What a tremendous amount of stress this put on their relationship. When one spouse is walking with God and the other isn't, it's always a struggle. Finally the Lord was disgusted with the people of Israel. He said to Moses, *"HOW LONG will these people reject me?"* *(Numbers 14:11a)*. God wanted Moses to separate himself from the people of Israel so He could deal harshly with their rebellion. This is why the Lord wants us to separate or divorce in these kinds of situations. He can only help so much while we are still attached. He cares about the helpless, the innocent and the righteous. We must decide whether we will follow God, or stay in the midst of the trouble. *"[For] God is jealous, and the Lord avenges" (Nahum 1:2a).*

God's original desire was to give everybody a possession in "the promised land." However, Moses didn't separate himself. Instead, he pleaded with God to forgive their sins and take them into the Promised Land, anyway. God pardoned their sins; but neither the children of Israel NOR Moses made it into the Promised Land. God let all the disobedient adults die out in the wilderness. Then He started all over with their children and two faithful adults (See Numbers 13,14 and Exodus 3:8).

When we purposely do contrary to God's will something happens in our heart. We seal rebellion in our hearts and therefore God's rejection. God is in the redemption business and reconciliation is always on His heart. However, when the rebellion is sealed in our heart we become untrustworthy. God will no longer include us in His redemption and reconciliation plan of saving others. Instead, He must now separate us from His plan, and focus His attention on saving us from ourselves — even if it means death. To die early and go to heaven is better than to live long and lose our place in God and go to hell. This is God's mercy.

The same promise He gave Moses is for us. God said, *"...and I WILL MAKE OF YOU a nation greater and mightier than they" (Numbers 14:12).* I believe the world missed out on one of the greatest opportunities. Had one man said, "Yes," Israel as a nation today could have been much greater and far more magnificent. God truly did promise, "I will make of you a nation greater and mightier than they."

GOD'S NATURE IS TO SEPARATE

God is a separator by nature. He Himself is *"...separate from sinners..." (Hebrews 7:26).*

When a person dies before they have ever confessed their sinfulness to God and have asked the Lord Jesus to come into their heart as Lord and Savior, they are forever separated from God, and damned to hell (See Mark 16:16).

When Jesus cast a demon out of a person, He said, *"...come out of him and ENTER HIM NO MORE!" (Mark 9:25).* Jesus separated that demon from that person forever, He said, "Enter (him) no more."

God is always in the process of separating. He's separating:
the **"good from evil"** *(1Peter 3:11),*

the **"holy from the unholy"**
(Leviticus 10:10),

the **"righteous from the unrighteous"**
(1Corinthians 6:9-10),

the **"wheat from the tares"**
(Matthew 13:24-30),

the **"sheep from the goats"**
(Matthew 25:31-46),

the **"light from the darkness"** *(Genesis 1:18).*
He calls us to separate: to *"have NO fellowship with the unfruitful works of darkness, but rather expose them" (Ephesians 5:11).*

Have you ever noticed that at certain times in our lives things just seem to flow? No matter what we do, it works out. That is called operating in or with the anointing. At other times it seems as if we're trying to push a stalled bulldozer. Despite how hard we try, things just don't work out. That is called operating without or against the anointing.

First, let me clarify what is the "anointing." An anointing is God's all-efficient means of enabling people to carry forth His purpose when called to do so. God has different kinds of anointings or enablements to accomplish specific tasks. Some anointings may only last minutes, others may last hours or days, while others may last months, years or even a lifetime, depending on what God's purpose is. For example, if the task is to prophecy or to encourage someone, the anointing may only last minutes. If it's to build a business, the anointing may last years.

There is an anointing God gives when "joining together" a couple and there's an anointing when God is "pulling apart" a couple (See Matthew 19:6, 10:34-37). These two anointings are apparent in the following Scriptures.

First, the anointing to separate: *"Do not think that I came to bring peace ...BUT A SWORD ...A man's enemies will be those of his own household. He who loves ...[even those of his own household] ...more than Me is not worthy of me" (Matthew 10:34-37).*

Second, the anointing to join together: *"For this reason a man shall ...be joined to his wife, and THE TWO SHALL BECOME ONE flesh. So then, they are no longer two, but one ...God has joined together..." (Matthew 19:5,6).*

In other words, **THERE'S AN ANOINTING IN MAKING THE "TWO INTO ONE," AND THERE'S AN ANOINTING TO SEPARATE OR DIVIDE THE "ONE INTO TWO."**

THE ANOINTING TO SEPARATE

Now you may say, "I could see why God anoints or enables the two to become one, but why is an anointing needed in pulling a marriage apart?" Let me start to answer that question with a question. Why do couples stay in dead relationships? Why are couples unable to leave their spouse when they are being abused? Why do wives keep buying the same old lie of "I'm sorry, forgive me" from their husbands when they find out he's molesting their daughter or when he's running around on her? Why? It's because they CAN'T break away. The couples have been "joined."

There are many areas of attachments in the joining of a couple. There are deep emotional bonds, physical and sexual bonds, social bonds, spiritual bonds, economical bonds, and so on. And because of these many attachments, God needs to send an anointing to divide the one back into two. Otherwise, the couple may never properly separate, but may continue to seek the other person out for any number of reasons and not know why. The Bible speaks about this power and ability of God's anointing: it's *"...living and powerful ...piercing even to the DIVISION OF SOUL AND SPIRIT ...and there is no creature hidden from His sight..." (Hebrews 4:12,13)*. There is nothing hidden from His sight. All of the bonds and attachments are visible to the anointing, even the emotions of your soul and the place in your spirits where you were made one. God knows how to separate; He knows how to do it properly, and He knows how to do it completely. Remember, when God separates a man from a woman by divorce, He separates once and for all time.

Whenever God separates a couple and that couple gets back together, they are in a marriage that's outside the will of God. The ordinance for that marriage has been annulled in God's heavenly books. Now, they are in an ungodly marriage. Repenting of daily living in a marriage that God does not approve of does not fix the problem, but repenting and getting out of the marriage does.

We often want God to bless our doings while we flagrantly disregard His will. Then we wonder why we can't get ahead in life. The only way to have God's best is to become fed up with our own efforts and be willing to accept His desires as our own. This may require us to back track to where we went off course. For instance, if we wronged someone, we must go back and be reconciled to them. If restitution is required, we must pay it. If it's a marriage or a relationship we are involved in outside of God's will and that's where we went off course, God may require us to separate. You must acknowledge that you have married someone against His will. You must ask Him for the anointing to dissolve the marriage (if that's what He wants) and to receive His strength to bring you through the separation. God requires us to fully pursue Him, which in turn may cause a separation in the

98

marriage <u>if the other spouse does not want to serve God and does not want you to serve God.</u>

This is the most painful part. We love God and don't want to leave Him but at the same time we are "attached" to our mate, not wanting to leave them despite what they do to us. This is the point where we need the anointing to help us separate, or else we may go on with our spouse and let our walk with God wane. Our life begins to become unsatisfying and we become miserable. Our desire for life becomes a daily chore. We wait for the day to be over in hopes of a better tomorrow. But that better tomorrow never seems to come. We wallow in memories of hurt and pain and the reality that we messed up. <u>There is hope</u>! God has not forgotten us. He is seeking us so He can restore our life even when we are not seeking Him.

MERCY AND JUDGMENT, THE BALANCE POINT

God is a lover of people (See John 3:16). *"[He] ...came into the world to SAVE sinners..." (1Timothy 1:15).* The attitude and motive of God's heart is to save. We must adopt this attitude and motive to properly discern whether our actions are of God or from ourselves. This is so we can tell if the marriage is being dissolved to save and preserve someone from another or if it is for selfish gain.

There is a nature of God that He reserves to Himself, and that's of judgment. You can't have true love without judgment. **TRUE LOVE ALWAYS HAS JUDGMENT.** God is balanced with love and judgment. Those who reject His love receive His judgment. But God wants us to have both His motive and attitude of love and be able to walk away from a situation without looking back when He begins the judgment process. This is essential.

This is the balance point of our Christian life. Because perfect love has judgment, <u>when mercy is exhausted</u>, we must expect God's judgment to come — even on ourselves. We are not to pray for God to judge someone, nor should we arbitrarily stand against it when judgment comes. But we must pray that the judgment will bring restoration. If we do not have the heart

99

of God in a critical situation such as this, we could actually be praying away the deliverance He sent to bring us to freedom. Many Christians lose their deliverance because of this very reason: they can't bear the pain of watching God deal with someone harshly, so they choose to stay in bondage for a lifetime instead of bearing the pain for a season (See Galatians 6:9).

Let me illustrate this in another way. The husband represents the nature of God's law and judgment. The wife represents and carries the nature of God's mercy and grace. The husband and wife marriage covenant is a representation of the love and judgment of God, even though "mercy triumphs over judgment" (See James 2:13b), **WHEN THE DEPTH OF MERCY HAS BEEN FULLY EXHAUSTED, MERCY MUST GIVE WAY TO JUDGMENT.**

DON'T LOOK BACK

Remember Lot's wife? The angels of the Lord said concerning the people of the cities of Sodom and Gomorrah, *"for we will destroy this place, because the outcry against them has grown great before the face of the Lord, and the Lord has sent us to destroy it" (Genesis 19:13).* Even though Abraham didn't want judgment to fall on the people, he let God have his way (See Genesis 19:17-33). When morning came, the angels said, *"Arise, take your wife and your two daughters who are here, LEST YOU BE CONSUMED IN THE PUNISHMENT of the city ...ESCAPE FOR YOUR LIFE! DO NOT LOOK BEHIND YOU NOR STAY ...But his wife looked back behind him, and she [Lot's wife] became a pillar of salt" (Genesis 19:15,17,26).*

God's judgment was present and God's mercy was present: judgment for those who rebelled against Him, and mercy for those who obeyed. But before God could bring mercy on whom mercy was due, and judgment on whom judgment was due, he had to first separate (divorce) the two, making them two separate entities, receiving each his own from God. God separated Lot's family from the ungodly so judgment wouldn't fall on them, only mercy. Judgment was reserved for the ungodly after they exhausted God's mercy. **FOR MERCY TRIUMPHS OVER JUDGMENT! BUT WHEN THE ABILITY OF MERCY HAS BEEN EXHAUSTED, MERCY GIVES WAY TO JUDGMENT** (See James 2:13).

You see, there are two ways to overcome evil: with love or with judgment. Evil is propagated through people. The Bible says to *"...overcome evil with good" (Romans 12:21)*. When we do good to someone doing evil to us, the love of God brings men to repentance. The love we show by doing good brings God's love to their heart. As they receive that love, they are changed. Evil has been overcome. But when that love is refused, there comes a time when judgment will step in to overcome the evil. When a person refuses the ability of the love of God to separate them from evil, they will perish along with the evil they embrace. **EVIL WILL BE OVERCOME WHETHER BY LOVE OR JUDGMENT** (See Romans 2:2-9).

IT'S GOOD TO SAVE PEOPLE

"A good man out of the good treasure of his heart brings forth good things, and an evil man out of the evil treasure of his heart brings forth evil things" (Matthew 12:35). When a desire comes from God, and flows through our heart, it is called "good treasure." And when the desire comes from satan, and flows through our heart, it is called "evil treasure."

When God is separating a couple to save a husband, wife or children from the corruption of the other spouse, it is called "good treasure." It is "good" to rescue a person from being destroyed. It seems that we want to save everything else these days, except people who need it the most. We want to save the whales; we want to save the dolphins; we want to save the fur-bearing animals; but we allow wives and children to get battered in their own homes. Something is very wrong with this picture! It's time to save the people of the marriage. *"For by GRACE you have been SAVED..." (Ephesians 2:8a)*.

Divorce in this case is the grace of God. We were saved out of a bad marriage. The Lord God says that it was good to save His people in old-covenant times who could not even be born again. It is written, *"Now therefore, make confession to the Lord God ...AND DO HIS WILL; SEPARATE YOURSELVES ...from the pagan wives" (Ezra 10:11).* How much more does the Lord love those who have been born of His Spirit? It is written, *"...keep yourselves in the love of God, LOOKING FOR THE MERCY OF THE LORD Jesus Christ ...PULLING THEM OUT OF THE FIRE, hating even the garment defiled by the flesh" (Jude 21,23).* A bad marriage is a tormenting fire.

THE BREAKING OF A "TIE," BECOMING TWO INSTEAD OF ONE

There is a traumatic effect when an intimate relationship is broken. It is one of the most painful experiences one may endure. That intimate "connecting" goes to the very depths of one's heart and soul. When there is a "tearing," it can greatly disrupt the entire life of a person. Fear not! We have an *"anchor of the soul, both sure and steadfast ...Jesus, [OUR] High Priest forever" (Hebrews 6:19,20).* He is able to pull us through unto Himself!

The Bible says, *"By faith we understand that the worlds were FRAMED by the Word of God..."(Hebrews 11:3).* When something is "framed," like a picture, it is "put together" and made complete. The framed picture becomes something different from the pieces that make it up. It becomes something new. The framed picture is now the whole, while the photo, the wood, glue and nails have lost their own identity as separate pieces. As we look closer at the picture frame, we see connections or "bridges" between the four corner joints. In a relationship, these bridges are called "soul-ties." They tie the husband and wife together. No longer are they identified as individuals, but *"...the TWO shall become ONE..." (Ephesians 5:31).* They have become something new, a family.

There are countless relationships that have been "legally" broken where one spouse can't help being drawn back to the other spouse. That's because their souls are still tied to their former spouse or lover. Another situation is where a spouse is unable to give himself or herself fully to the other. The problem is a "scattered soul." Both of these situations are caused from soul-ties that have never been broken. Even though a soul-tie that existed by law was broken when the marriage certificate was cancelled as a result of a certificate of divorce, there still must be a breaking or separating of the soul and spirit.

For the sake of discussion, the terms, "soul-tie," "double-minded," "scattered soul" and "divided soul" will be used interchangeably.

A "double-minded" person is a person with a divided soul (See James 1:8). When one's soul is divided, *"...let not that man suppose that he will receive anything from the Lord" (James 1:7).* We can give and give and give into our marriage but it seems as though we get very little in return. **HAVING A SCATTERED, DIVIDED SOUL, AFFECTS OUR RECEIVING, NOT OUR GIVING**. *"For let not that man suppose that he will RECEIVE anything..." (James 1:7).* When our soul is divided, it affects our receiving, not our giving. We may wonder why we can't receive the love and affection from our spouse that we so desperately need. They tell us that they love us, but somehow it's not getting through to us. We then conclude, because of our inability to receive, that our spouse is not really "giving" us the affection we need. Untold marriages have unnecessarily failed because of this very reason.

We can see how this seriously affects our trust for the other person. They say they love us, but because we are unable to receive that love, we unconsciously deem them untrustworthy because we are not receiving what they say they are giving. You can see how a person who is double-minded has relationship problems, including their relationship with God.

The Bible says, *"If any of you lacks wisdom, let him ASK of God, who gives..." (James 1:5).* Because we can't receive what we ask for, we believe that it has never been given, when in fact, it has. So our receiving or rather our inability to receive is based on our soul being tied to someone. In other words, we receive from the person with whom we have soul-ties. A soul-tie is a connection of the heart (See Hebrews 4:12). There are good soul-ties and bad soul-ties. There are soul-ties that produce life in us, and there are soul-ties that produce death in us. God wants us to break the soul-ties that produce death.

BREAKING FREE

A scattered soul will actually keep us from giving ourselves fully to our mate. If someone has three sexual relations including the relation with their current husband or wife, that would mean that 66% of the person's heart is tied to someone else. Of course, this is not a direct mathematical equation, but you get my point. The person can't give 100% of themselves to the other person because they don't have 100% to give, only 33%. This heart deficiency continues until the soul-ties are broken, and that part of our heart reclaimed. Breaking these soul-ties with the person you're being divorced from is necessary to be truly free. Breaking the soul-ties of those old relationships can actually save your marriage. Now you are able to freely love your mate with ALL of your heart.

Having a divided soul has primarily two deep-rooted negative effects in relationships. First, it hinders our ability to receive. In other words, the affection that is being given to us does not appear to reach our heart. Second, the capacity in which you can give is limited. Even though we give all our heart, we have only a portion to give. You can only give what's yours to give. A divided soul does not affect your giving, but it does affect HOW MUCH you have to give.

How are soul-ties formed, and how do we break them? Soul-ties are formed many different ways, and these are just a few of them: by willing or forced sexual relations (See Matthew 19:5,6, Genesis 24:67, 1Corinthians 6:16), by speaking words of commitment — vows: "I will always love you," "I will never forget," "I will always hate you," becoming soul brothers with someone (See 1Samuel 18:1), by receiving a ring (or item) from someone that represents a covenant agreement. And what I consider to be the most devious method of all is when you are given an item from a friend or relative that has great sentimental value but is, literally, death. Such as items that have been used in witchcraft or the occult. These kinds of soul-ties are ties to curses. Of course, there are also soul-ties to blessings, but these are not our discussion.

When someone says to us, "This piece of jewelry has been passed down from your great, great Aunt Millie, and I want you to have it," BEWARE! The devil knows that people (especially females) are sentimental people. If the devil can pass on something that has been used for his purpose, he knows we won't throw it away and the curse will continue. When there is sentimental value on something, it blinds our eyes (for good or bad) so we will not receive anything bad about that person. Of course, the devil knows that, for it's one of his prized schemes to keep us tied to the wrong people, or have bad things happen in our life.

There are various other ways for soul-ties to be formed and much to be learned. In the SOURCES section at the rear of this book I make reference of some books that will help you on this subject.

All soul-ties aren't bad and some are essential. We want our souls fully tied to Christ. We renew and strengthen that tie by communion and walking by His Spirit. We want to be "one mind" with the Lord (See 1Corinthians 2:16, Philippians 4:2). We also want and need this oneness with our mate, being *"...no longer two but ONE..." (Matthew 19:6).*

Breaking soul-ties and curses is done from the heart, with the mouth, and with the blood and name of Jesus (See Romans 10:9-10, Revelation 12:11). Be sure your heart is clean before breaking soul-ties and curses. If it's not, ask the Lord Jesus to forgive you and the other person of those specific sins: such as the sin of willingly having sex with someone when it was wrong.

Because each situation is different, a "one prayer fits all" is not possible. Here is a sample prayer of repentance and how to break and renounce the curses and soul-ties:

"Lord Jesus, I ask you to forgive me of all my sins regarding these soul-ties and curses (name them). In the name of Jesus I renounce, cover with the blood of Jesus, and break off from my family and me all soul-ties, curses and relationships regarding (name the person(s). I ask you, Lord Jesus, to free me and cleanse me from all those deep-rooted ties and curses."

If you have a piece of jewelry or something from that person, hold it and speak over it, "I break and renounce all covenants and relationships that were sealed by this item (name the item) that they (name the person) gave me, and now I reclaim and surrender these parts of my life to Your lordship, dear Jesus."

Now, get rid of the item. The Lord spoke to the heart of someone I know concerning this matter. He said, "Break it. If it won't break, burn it, and if it won't burn, bury it!" These Scriptures bear this truth out (See Deuteronomy 7:4,5,25,26 and Isaiah 2:17-21).

6

Marriage, Remarriage And Relationship

DIVORCE AND REMARRIAGE

"Now the Spirit [of God] expressly says that in latter times [the days we live in now] some will DEPART FROM THE FAITH, giving heed to deceiving spirits and doctrines of demons, speaking lies ...FORBIDDING TO MARRY..." (1 Timothy 4:1,3).

"...Rejoice before Him. [For] GOD SETS THE SOLITARY [Those who are without parent or spouse] IN FAMILIES; [and] HE BRINGS OUT THOSE WHO ARE BOUND [whether by drugs or a bad marriage] INTO PROSPERITY..." (Psalm 68:5,6).

"Forbidding [someone] to marry" after they have been divorced is a doctrine of the devil. The Bible is not saying that these people who hold to this belief are not true Christians, but that they teach out of ignorance — they don't understand God's heart in the Scriptures. Understanding God's heart only comes from the Holy Spirit revealing Him to us. Whenever we do not understand God's heart in the Scriptures, we have departed from sound doctrine.

This Scripture could not be talking about forbidding to marry in general. Nobody would listen to such nonsense preached. The desire that God put in man to have a companion and sexual partner is too great, especially if they were married before. In order that we don't fall into *"...sexual immorality, let EACH MAN have his own wife, and let EACH WOMAN have her own husband." "[For] IT IS NOT GOOD THAT MAN SHOULD BE ALONE..." (1 Corinthians 7:2, Genesis 2:18a).*

The erroneous doctrine of forbidding one to marry after a divorce has been preached and taught in many churches. It has violated the conscience and hearts of those who've been divorced, driving them into a constant state of confusion and negatively impacting their lives. The only way for these people to come out of that confused state is to leave the church, and many have done just that. Not only do they leave the church to remarry, they also need to be able to make the right decision to divorce when it's necessary in order to save themselves and their families before all is destroyed.

In order to understand that there IS marriage after divorce, we will examine the Scriptures in Matthew 19:3-12 focusing on the usage of the Greek word, *apoluo*. The Greek word *apoluo* that's translated "divorce" or to "put away" is a general word. Its primary usage is: to "send" *(apoluo)* someone home when it's getting late.[11] When two people are leaving each other there is a "separation." The Old Testament Hebrew word *shalach* and the New Testament Greek word *apoluo* are equivalent as discussed earlier. *Apoluo* is a separation in general, which does not involve the "legal" aspect of a permanent separation like a divorce. The common usage is seen in the Scripture *"When it was evening, His disciples came to Him, saying 'This is a deserted place, and the hour is already late. SEND (apoluo) the multitudes away, that they may go unto the villages and buy themselves food'" (Matthew 14:15).* The Greek word *apoluo* doesn't have a legal aspect to it. It's just a common word that means, "I'm going to go" or, "away from, to separate." As previously taught, the Old Testament Hebrew word *shalach* is the equivalent to the New Testament Greek word *apoluo*. Their just common words that mean to: go, send or separate from. Because of our wrong beliefs about divorce, this key word was purposely translated (incorrectly) so it would not conflict with our beliefs.

When used concerning a marriage it means a separation and NOT a divorce. If a spouse separates intending never to return, then the next step comes into play; the spouse obtains a "certificate of divorce." This is what the confrontation between Jesus and the Pharisees (the religious lawyers of His day) was about in Matthew 19:3-12. The legal question was, "Do you just separate, OR do you separate AND give a certificate of divorce?" The Greek word used for divorce in these Scriptures means, to "send away" or separate from, NOT a finalized legal divorce.

The lawyers of God's law tested Jesus. Their motive was to justify when they only separated from their wives and remarried without ever getting a divorce. They asked Him if God accepts a separation to get remarried without a divorce certificate for just any reason. Jesus responded that when a male and female come together in a marriage union, "...*they are no longer two BUT ONE..." (Matthew 19:6a).* Because the couple is still united, He doesn't want "man" (the marriage partners) to just separate from each other and get remarried without a divorce. **A SEPARATION ALONE DOES *NOT* BE MARRIAGE UNION. IT TAKES A CERTIFICATE OF ALSO.** So the question was NOT, "Can a spouse DIV mate for any reason," but "Can a spouse get a SE from their mate for any reason and then remarry separated and not divorced." (A complete translation of these Scriptures with the correct words can be found in the rear of this book in the APPENDIX section.)

When a husband just leaves his wife for another woman without ever giving her a certificate of divorce, this keeps the wife in limbo. She could not go back to her husband because he doesn't want her; and she couldn't "go and become another man's wife" as Moses commanded because she is not legally divorced (See Deuteronomy 24:1-2). If she did remarry without a legal divorce, she and the man who married her would be committing adultery. This is why Jesus said, *"...whoever separates (apoluo) from his wife, except for sexual immorality, and marries another, commits adultery; and whoever marries her who is [just] separated (apoluo) commits adultery"* (Matthew 19:9 *My Translation).*

Because the Pharisees' hearts were so hard *"They said to Him [Jesus], 'WHY then did Moses COMMAND to give a certificate of divorce AND to put her away [separate]?'"* (Matthew 19:7). They agreed with the part of the law that said that you could leave your wife, but they didn't understand that it was not right to keep their wives from getting remarried. A spouse with a hardened heart will not give the other spouse a divorce. They will want to control the person. A person who truly loves without selfishness will always give you a way out: an option not to love.

So it is with God; He always gives us the choice to not love Him. As we choose to love Him, it's true love. At times the reason a marriage isn't a truly committed loving marriage is because the partners feel that there is never a way out, if needed. If the marriage partners knew that there was a godly way to escape from a failing marriage it would give the couple the freedom to "choose to love," even when it's not convenient.

Jesus said to them, *"Moses, because of the hardness of your hearts, PERMITTED you to divorce [separate from] your wives, but from the beginning IT [being separated without a*

,)orce] WAS NOT SO" (Matthew 19:8). Notice in verse seven that Moses COMMANDED them to give a certificate of divorce AND to separate (put away) their wives. But in verse eight, because their hearts were so hardened against their spouse, Moses PERMITTED them to just separate without the husband giving the wife a certificate of divorce. The reason Moses commanded that a certificate of divorce be given was to guarantee that the wife could get remarried. Simply, Moses commanded to give a certificate of divorce AND to separate. But because of the hardness of their hearts, Moses permitted them to separate only. The permission to separate and remarry without a divorce was limited to sexual immorality. If the wife was unfaithful, the husband could leave without ever being "officially divorced" — by giving her a certificate of divorcement, and go take another woman as his wife. But if there was no sexual immorality involved, the husband could NOT separate from his wife without getting a divorce first. If he didn't get a divorce and went to live with another woman or got remarried, they were committing adultery.

"Are you bound to a wife? Do not seek to be loosed [for selfish reasons]. Are you loosed [divorced] from a wife? [In my opinion says Paul, the Apostle] do not seek a wife. BUT EVEN IF YOU DO MARRY, YOU HAVE NOT SINNED; and if a virgin marries, she has not sinned" (1Corinthians 7:26-28a). Notice that the "virgin" AND the person "loosed [divorced]" are both put in the same category — they have "not sinned" by getting married. **BOTH THE PERSON WHO WAS NEVER MARRIED AND THE PERSON WHO WAS DIVORCED ARE WITHOUT SIN IF THEY MARRY.**

Deuteronomy 24:1-4 tells of a situation where a man married a woman and then divorced her. This woman then married another man. The Scriptures go on to state that if the second marriage ends by her husband writing "...her a certificate of divorce ...OR if the latter husband dies..." (Deuteronomy 24:3,4), she could not remarry the first man she divorced because she had already married someone else. Therefore, if our spouse dies, or if we were divorced, we can get married again. Divorce and death are equal before God. The only stipulation in this Scripture is that if this is the second marriage, we cannot go back to the first spouse and remarry them because we married someone else after we divorced them.

REMARRIAGE TRUTH

In 1Corinthians 7:27,28 it says, *"Are you bound to a wife? Do not seek to be loosed. Are you loosed from a wife? Do not seek a wife. But even if you do marry, you have not sinned."*

What we have been taught is that you can ONLY get remarried if your spouse is dead — period! Therefore, let's apply this teaching to this scripture. *"Are you bound (married) to a wife? Do not seek be loosed (to kill her or to put a contract out on her). Are you loosed from a wife (did you kill her or have her murdered)? Do not seek a wife. But even if you do marry another woman (after you had your wife killed) you have not sinned."* Can you see the utter silliness of that rationale? This is the proper understanding: *"Are you bound (married) to a wife? Do not seek to be loosed (divorced). Are you loosed (divorced) from a wife? Do not seek a wife. But even if you do marry (after you have been divorced), you have not sinned."*

Next, direct your attention to 1Corinthians 7:8,9 which says, *"I say unto the UNMARRIED and the WIDOWS, 'it is good for them if they abide even as I (meaning to stay single). But if THEY cannot contain (having self-control to stay single) LET THEM MARRY: FOR IT IS BETTER TO MARRY than to burn (with passion for a mate).'"*

Religion has taught us that the "unmarried" in this Scripture does not refer to anyone who was divorced, only to those who where NEVER MARRIED. If "unmarried" means "NEVER MARRIED," then why did Paul the Apostle who wrote this letter continuing only sixteen verses later say, "NOW concerning VIRGINS...???" Virgins (those who where NEVER MARRIED were NOT of those mentioned who where UNMARRIED. "NOW" he is talking about them — the virgins. Before he wasn't! Then Paul goes on to say that the virgins and those who are UNMARRIED —"loosed from a wife" (divorced) are in the same category if they marry — "THEY HAVE NOT SINNED."

Therefore, 1Corinthians 7:27,28 properly reads: *"Are you bound (married) to a wife? Do not seek to be loosed (divorced). Are you loosed (divorced) from a wife? Do not seek a wife. But even if you do marry (after you have been divorced), you have not sinned; and if a virgin marries, she has not sinned."*

ADULTERY, GROUNDS FOR DIVORCE?

Again, the Son of God confronted the hardness of heart of the religious leaders. This time, they dragged into the temple (the church building) someone's wife who was caught in the very act of adultery. (I wonder why the man wasn't brought in, too)? This incident took place in John 8:1-11.

After the accusations and indictments have been hurled out, Jesus said, *"He who is without sin among you, let him throw a stone at her first" (John 8:7).* Jesus then stooped down again and wrote in the dirt. When He stood up, every one of her accusers were gone, and not a stone was thrown. He said to her, *"'Woman, where are those accusers of yours? Has no one condemned you?' She said, 'No one, Lord'. And Jesus said to her, 'Neither do I condemn you; GO and sin no more'" (John 8:10-11).*

Go where? Go back to her husband and be the kind of wife that God wants her to be. Jesus did not say that adultery was grounds for divorce. He did not even tell her to make it right with her husband, even though she may have been convicted to do just that. But Jesus did say, *"Neither do I condemn you; GO AND SIN NO MORE" (John 8:11).*

The religious leaders said that she should be stoned to death for adultery, NOT DIVORCED! Because there are different situations and circumstances in which adultery is committed, there are different laws for each situation. The stoning punishment that they applied was for a "betrothed damsel" — an engaged woman who was never married. This was spelled out in Deuteronomy 22:24 and Leviticus 20:10. It appeared that Jesus applied the law of Numbers 5:11-31 where adultery is committed in secret and because this woman was "another man's wife." In this case the wife was to be taken to the Priest. The curses were pronounced and written down regarding her supposed sinfulness. She was then to drink a certain mixture prepared by the Priest and then to say, "Amen, so be it." She was then able to leave and the punishment was left up to God according to what was written. This is probably why Jesus was writing in the dirt — the curses of the sin. But Jesus showed mercy. Even though there are consequences, He wanted to forgive and to cleanse.

ADULTERY IS NOT A *MANDATORY* REASON FOR A DIVORCE. If it were, that would mean that we could, according to Jesus, divorce our spouse if they only committed the act of adultery in their heart. Jesus said, *"You have heard that it was said to those of old, 'you shall not commit adultery.' But I say to you that WHOEVER LOOKS AT A WOMAN TO LUST for her HAS ALREADY COMMITTED ADULTERY WITH HER IN HIS HEART"* *(Matthew 5:27,28).*

If we never had physical sexual contact with anybody outside of our marriage but we committed "adultery in our heart" would this be ground for a divorce? If it were, there probably wouldn't be a person alive who would still be married. Jesus was saying to keep our minds clean just as we would keep our bodies clean. The issue was not that adultery was mandatory grounds for divorce. The issue was that a hard-hearted person could leave his spouse without giving them an actual legal divorce. The unforgiveness in them may be so deep that they would fight the divorce so that their spouse might never enjoy being married to another person. In this case, Moses gave them "permission" to separate without a divorce on one condition: physical adultery.

They Say, "We Have A Spouse," Yet We're Unmarried

Again, because we have applied our beliefs to the interpretation and translation of the Scriptures another Truth has been clothed with man's traditions. We have been incorrectly taught that once a person is divorced, they somehow still have a spouse. They cannot get married again.

We have been told that a person cannot get married once they have been divorced because their spouse is alive, even though after the divorce they don't have a spouse; but once that spouse dies, they can then get married. In the case of the woman who was divorced, it is NOT true that her HUSBAND is alive, but it IS true that her FORMER HUSBAND is alive. To put it another way, we were told that we were "bound" (married) to someone when we weren't. We were quoted that *"a wife is BOUND by law as long as her husband lives [that's if she has one, but a divorced woman doesn't have a husband]; but if her husband dies, she is at liberty to be married to whom she wishes, only in the Lord"* (1 Corinthians 7:39). This isolated Scripture was used as an illustration by the Apostle Paul to give an example of when a person dies; they are no longer under the law. Paul was NOT teaching about divorce.

How then can we accept that we have a spouse when we're not married? When a person is divorced, they don't have a husband or wife. This means they are not "bound" to someone. This Scripture is for the person who is MARRIED and wants to marry someone else while they are still married to another. You can't be married to two people at the same time. If you're divorced, you CAN get married again because you don't have a husband or wife. Simply, you're single or unmarried, if divorced.

"I say to the UNMARRIED and widows: It is good for them if they remain even as I [the Apostle Paul] am; but if they cannot exercise self-control, LET THEM MARRY. FOR IT IS BETTER TO MARRY THAN TO BURN WITH PASSION" (1 Corinthians 7:8,9). Who would "burn with passion" the most: the person who was NEVER married, who never knew a close intimate relationship and the pleasures of sex, or the person who had been married? God knows the power and pull that a sexually intimate relationship has on a person once they are separated from their spouse. That's why He said concerning prayer and fasting, *"Do not deprive one another [sexually] except with consent for a time, that you may give yourself to fasting and prayer; AND COME TOGETHER AGAIN SO THAT SATAN DOES NOT TEMPT YOU BECAUSE OF YOUR LACK OF SELF-CONTROL"* (1 Corinthians 7:5).

THE TRUE WIDOW

The reason that the church in general has blackballed those who have gone through a divorce is because they do not categorize them properly. This is done through misunderstanding of the Scriptures.

The Bible says there are *"...the unmarried ...the widows ...[and] the married..." (1Corinthians 7:8-10)*. The "married" are just that: a man and a woman together in a marriage union. The "unmarried" (which is a general term) are those who are not married: those who were never married, and those who were divorced or never remarried. "Widows" are those who have been married but now do not have a husband because of death or divorce. **IN GOD'S EYES, DIVORCE AND DEATH ARE EQUAL.**

Because this ministry to the widow is so greatly neglected and misunderstood by the church, yet so dearly loved by God, it is best to establish what qualifies a woman as a widow.

Webster's American Family Dictionary defines widow, grass widow, divorce and widowhood, as:

Widow: "A woman who has lost her husband by death and has not remarried."[12]

Grass widow: "A woman who is separated, divorced or lives apart from her husband."[13]

Divorced: "A judicial declaration dissolving a marriage and releasing both spouses from all matrimonial obligations."[14]

Widowhood: "The state or period of being a widow or, sometimes, a widower."[15]

As used in the Bible, "widowhood" and "widow," are both from one Hebrew word, *alman,* which means "discarded (as a divorced person), forsaken."[16]

The root meaning of being a "widow" is that you are divorced or forsaken by your husband. The method by which the spouse is left without a husband is immaterial.

In the Bible, when a woman identified herself as a widow, depending for what purpose, she indicated specifically HOW she was widowed. For instance, in 2Samual 14:5, as a woman addresses the king, she said, *"I am a WIDOW woman, AND MINE HUSBAND IS DEAD" (KJV)*. Being a widow meant more than being without a husband. It meant you had a husband but he either died, he deserted you, or you were divorced. This woman had to be specific in identifying how she was widowed to the king. If being a widow did not include being a divorced person as well, it would have been very foolish for her to say, "My husband is dead and my husband is dead." That's what it would have sounded like to the king, if "widow" only meant "my husband is dead."

That woman experienced widowhood because her husband died. In the next situation, these women experienced widowhood WHILE THEIR FORMER HUSBANDS WERE STILL ALIVE.

Again, the king was involved. This time, it was not a widow addressing him, but he was making his concubines into "widows." *"And the king took the ten women, his concubines whom he had left to keep the house, and put them in seclusion and supported them, but did not go in to them. So they were shut up to the day of their death, LIVING IN WIDOWHOOD" (2Samuel 20:3)*. These women, being separated from their husband David, became widows while David was STILL ALIVE.

Widowhood has the connotation of the breaking of the "sex union" by death, divorce or desertion. For King David "did not go in to them." A marriage is more than just living under the same roof together; it's a loving and physical relationship with our spouse. For *"...they are NO LONGER TWO but one flesh" (Matthew. 19:6a)*.

TWO TYPES OF WIDOWS

The two types of widows are: a woman whose husband is dead, and a woman whose former husband is alive are. BOTH are revealed in 1Timothy chapter 5.

Paul the Apostle, writing to Timothy, is giving him instructions concerning what KIND OF WIDOW is to be given priority in receiving financial help and care from the church. He starts off by saying, *"Honor widows who are REALLY WIDOWS"* *(1Timothy 5:3)*. Being a widow means you have been forsaken by your husband. Being one of those who are "really widows" means that your husband has forsaken you AND you do not have a source of supply: no alimony, no pension, no parents to help, or no children to help.

There are widows who have children and grandchildren. The Apostle said to, *"let THEM (the children and grandchildren) first learn to show piety at home and to REPAY THEIR PARENTS; for this is good and acceptable before God"* *(1Timothy 5:5)*.

The Apostle goes on to say, *"If any believing man or woman has WIDOWS, let them (the parents professing to be Christians) relieve them, and do not let the church be burdened, that it may relieve those who are really widows"* *(1Timothy 5:16)*.

Notice that instead of being an elderly widow with children and grandchildren (meaning that the widow's parents are probably deceased), THESE "widows" have a mother and/or father. A mother and/or father can have MULTIPLE widows. In other words, the parents may have several daughters who were divorced from their husbands. In this case, it is the parent's responsibility to help their widowed (divorced) children.

God's heart is for the widow whether it be the widow woman mentioned in 2Samuel 14:5 whose alleged husband died, or King David's widows in 2Samuel 20:3c who were living in widowhood while their husbands were still alive, or the woman that God used as an example in Deuteronomy 24:3,4 who was divorced from her husband, or you. God said if someone is afflicting them *"...and thy cry AT ALL to Me, I will surely hear their cry" (Exodus 22:23).* Widows have a special place in God's heart.

The Scriptures in Acts 9:36-42 tell of a lady named Tabitha who was also called Dorcas. She was full of good works and charitable deeds. Her ministry was in helping the widows by practical means. The Scriptures do not specify whether her husband divorced her or if he died. Because she has suffered the same pain and struggle as other widows, she had the compassion to minister to those with the same hurts. When we work through our sufferings, it produces compassion and grace in us for others who hurt in the same way. Tabitha was probably a widow herself.

It happened that Tabitha became sick and died. As they prepared her body for the funeral, some of her friends went to get Peter the Apostle to pray because they heard he was in town. When Peter arrived, they took him to the funeral. The people who came to see her at the funeral were those to whom she had ministered. *"And ALL THE WIDOWS stood by him weeping, showing the tunics [undershirts] and [other] garments which Dorcas had made WHILE SHE WAS WITH THEM" (Acts 9:39c).* After Peter put them all out of the room, he prayed to God, and then said to the dead woman, *"...Tabitha, arise. And she opened her eyes ...[and] sat up" (Acts 9:40).*

God in His graciousness felt it worthy to raise Tabitha from the dead so that she could continue in the precious ministry He had given to her. He truly is *"...a defender of widows..." (Psalm 68:5).*

THE SABBATHS OF THE LORD

God was very angry with His people Israel. He had Ezekiel the prophet tell the Israelites that He was sending "the Sword of the Lord" after them because of their sins. God called Israel a *"...BLOODY CITY... [For] ...in your midst they have OPPRESSED THE STRANGER; in you they have MISTREATED THE FATHERLESS AND THE WIDOW. You have despised my holy things and PROFANED MY SABBATHS. ...And they [the*

120

princes of Israel] have hidden their eyes from MY SABBATHS, SO THAT I AM PROFANED AMONG THEM" (Ezekiel 22:2,7,8,26c).

The "Sabbaths" are the "stranger," the "fatherless," and the "widow." And God said that He was profaned amongst THEM: the Sabbaths!

The Hebrew word "sabbath(s)" means an "intermission, repose (rest, calm), desist." [17] When the word sabbath(s) is used pertaining to a "day," as "the Sabbath day or Sabbaths," it means the day of rest, the day of intermission, the day that we desist from our normal daily activities.

When the word sabbath(s) is used pertaining to a person, such as the stranger, the fatherless or the widow, it reveals the break in THEIR normal lives. The stranger is a sabbath because he or she has desisted from being in their own city and home and have gone to another; the fatherless is a sabbath because he or she has desisted from having a father; the widow is a sabbath because she desisted from having a husband, whether by divorce or death. For that reason, God said, *"...[That if] THEY cry at all to Me, I WILL SURELY HEAR THEIR CRY; and My wrath will become hot..." (Exodus 22:23,24).*

The leadership of Israel, like the church today, did not represent God properly before the stranger, the fatherless and the widow. They profaned God. They made His Word and His love of no effect in their lives. They exalted the laws of God higher than having a loving relationship with the Lawgiver Himself. They no longer believed that God was *"A father of the fatherless, a DEFENDER OF WIDOWS, ...[and that] God in His holy habitation ...SETS THE SOLITARY [Those who are without parent or spouse] IN FAMILIES; [and] HE BRINGS OUT THOSE WHO ARE BOUND [Whether by drugs or a bad marriage] INTO PROSPERITY..." (Psalm 68:5,6).*

Church of God, our Father, the God of heaven and of earth, has made a place for us in His kingdom. But if we forget that we *"...shall not afflict ANY widow or fatherless child ...[OR] ...afflict them in ANY way..."* then our very Father and God whom we say we love, will become our disciplinary. *"...[For if] THEY cry at all to Me, I WILL SURELY HEAR THEIR CRY; and My wrath will become hot, and I will kill you with the sword; YOUR*

121

wives shall be widows, and YOUR children fatherless" (Exodus 22:22-24).

How many times has God's discipline been on a local church because of the way they have treated the stranger, the fatherless, and those who were widowed or divorced? God knows what it's like for a stranger not to feel welcome. He knows how the fatherless miss the feel of the strong arms of a loving father. He understands the deep heartache and void left in a person after the spouse leaves them or dies. He knows the pain. He has taken up their cause and said, *"...ASSURELY, I say to you, inasmuch as you did it to one of the least of these my brethren, you did it to Me" (Matthew 25:40).*

Some of the causes that the Lord has taken up in behalf of the strangers, fatherless, and widows, are: God has commanded US to give them food from the crops of our land (See Deuteronomy 24:19-22), to give them a portion of OUR financial income, which is called tithes and offerings (See Deuteronomy 26:12,13), and not to pervert justice that's due them. Otherwise we fall under a curse (See Deuteronomy 27:19). He relieves them of being fatherless or of being a widow (See Psalm 146:9). He commands US to do good and to defend His Sabbaths (See Isaiah 1:17,23), and to do them no wrong (See Jeremiah 22:3).

These people are so precious in God's sight that He DEMANDS for us to take up their cause. The Lord came *"...to set at liberty those who are oppressed..." (Luke 4:18b),* no matter how that oppression may be manifested: a bad marriage, or a bad habit. He came *"...to PROCLAIM LIBERTY TO THE CAPTIVES..." (Luke 4:18b).*

The heart of God is truly expressed through Job. Even though Job went through what appeared to be hell, he cried out from deep within himself and said, *"...I CAUSED THE WIDOW'S HEART TO SING FOR JOY" (Job 29:13b).* No wonder God loved Job so much; Job took up the causes of God's heart for His sabbaths.

LED BY THE SPIRIT THROUGH A DIVORCE

We ask God to help us choose a mate and then ask for His help to work things out when we are newly married. After we've been married awhile, it often seems like God is left out of the picture. It may be because we are too embarrassed to include Him in our daily activities because of our mate. Perhaps we have left our first love and esteemed the relationship with our spouse higher than our relationship with God. In either case, we have forgotten that God was with us in the marriage. We must not forget our loving God as part of our daily lives. He tenderly cares for us.

We must not forget God is with us when He's getting us out of a marriage. This may seem confusing, but remember: if God is FOR the marriage, He will lead you INTO it; if God is FOR the divorce, He will lead you OUT of the marriage. If God is against a marriage or a divorce, He will lead you away from it. In all situations, He will lead you to Himself so you can find His heart on the matter if you seek Him.

Being led by the Spirit of God through a divorce is crucial. There are many steps the Lord will take a spouse through as He leads them through a divorce. Maybe it's praying to know the right timing of the divorce itself. Maybe it's deciding which spouse will actually do the divorcing or who will physically stay in the house and who will leave. We need to pray with right motives. We need to have forgiveness in our heart toward our spouse. We need daily direction from God for all those major decisions both before and after the final separation. Most importantly, we need to receive the deep work that God wants to do in our own heart so we don't repeat old sins and mistakes but become changed more and more into His likeness.

God wants to direct ALL of our life. For *"in ALL your ways acknowledge Him, and He shall direct [ALL] your paths" (Proverbs 3:6).*

Not only did Jesus die and rise from the dead for our sin nature that keeps people out of heaven, but He also died so we can have a happy marriage. For *"SURELY He (Jesus) has borne our griefs and carried our sorrows..." (Isaiah 53:4)* for our

123

marriages, so that *"when you eat the labor of your hands, YOU SHALL BE HAPPY, AND IT SHALL BE WELL WITH YOU. YOUR WIFE SHALL BE LIKE A FRUITFUL VINE IN THE VERY HEART OF YOUR HOUSE..." (Psalm 128:2,3)*. That sounds like a happy marriage to me. It may be hard to believe, but God truly does want us to have a happy and joy-filled marriage more than we want one. However, He won't force us to love Him, nor can we force our mate to love God. We always have to make that choice for ourselves.

Being led by the Spirit of God through a divorce will leave us free and at peace. When we go through a divorce being led by what is called "the flesh," we will not be at peace or rest. On the contrary, we may be legally divorced but we will still be bound by unforgiveness, resentment, anger and blame. As the Spirit of God leads us out of the marriage, He will lead us to *"...bless those who curse you, [and to] do good to those who hate you, and [to] pray for those who spitefully use you and persecute you" (Matthew 5:44)*. As we willfully do these actions our heart will be transformed, enabling us to walk in love for those who hate the very ground we walk on.

Being led out of the marriage by the flesh (which is bitterness, resentment, anger, unforgiveness, and other wrong attitudes and motives) will cause our heart to change also. The change will not be for the better, but for the worse. The difference between those who have gone through traumatic emotional situations whose hearts are now healed and those whose hearts aren't, is that the one who is healed worked through their pain with God. The one who is not healed did not work through their pain even though they may know God personally. That is the reason some people will not take peace and a changed heart to their new marriage. The prime reason we don't work through the pain of those damaged areas of our heart is because the road to healing and wholeness seems to hurt more than the traumatic incident(s) we experienced. If we will not allow the time, exercise courage with focused determination to press on to wholeness despite the pain we feel, the next marriage will end in divorce or fall far short of the happiness and joy that a marriage can bring. We must allow God to do His full work in our heart no matter how long it takes or how much it hurts. Then we will find ourselves gradually rejoicing in the ongoing change that God is secretly doing inside.

Relationship In Marriage

You may believe that only "good feelings" toward each other will keep the marriage relationship strong. This belief is disproved the very first time a problem arises in the relationship. **FEELINGS THAT LAST ARE BORN FROM A PRICE THAT WAS PAID.** That's what "laying down one's life for another" is all about.

A marriage is much more than two people living together. It's more than two people living together and having sex. It's relationship — relating to each other. It's a relationship between couples that is built over time, beginning before AND continuing after the marriage ceremony.

When a man and a woman go through a marriage ceremony, God places upon them a debt they must pay. The debt is to *"owe no one anything EXCEPT to love [them]..." (Romans 13:8).* If there is anything of value that a husband and wife must owe to each other, it is to love. Love is the very foundation of a marriage relationship. (The four types of love will be discussed later.) It is the base upon which two people share an entire life together. Without the giving and receiving of love between a husband and wife, the marriage relationship becomes mechanical and without meaning. The institution of marriage without love becomes an empty shell. When that institution is filled with love, it becomes a vibrant living thing that's beautiful to behold and a joy to the couple.

God Himself ordained the marriage institution and set a specific order within the home. Over the past few years, God has been revealing to me what I call, "a kingdom family." This loving kingdom family existed in God's heart from the beginning. It's the reason He created man. As a result of sin entering man through rebellion, the fullness of the nature of the kingdom family has not yet been fully seen in the earth. A major part of this lack of love in the family is because of the man's failure as a husband. The husband has a vital role in producing love, which is God's nature, in a family. Because *"...the husband is head of the wife, AS ALSO Christ is head of the church..." (Ephesians 5:23),* a great responsibility is placed upon him by God to lay down his life for his family.

As I was walking, seeking God late one night, He revealed to me that the continual flow of love that's needed between a husband and wife starts with the husband. Let me explain. The number one need of a man is companionship: having his wife as his playmate in those things that interest HIM and give HIM relaxation and pleasure. But that is NOT the number one need of a woman. The number one need of a woman is affection. Because the number one needs are different for a man and a woman, it presents a problem. That is, if a husband naturally expresses himself to his wife, he will overlook her needs to fulfill his own. And if a wife naturally expresses herself to her husband, she will overlook his needs to fulfill her own. **A MARRIAGE RELATIONSHIP IS BASED UPON SOMEONE GIVING UP HIS/HER NUMBER ONE NEED TO SATISFY THE NEED OF THE OTHER.**

God said to me, *"Son, My Son gave up His number one need for His bride, the church."* Then God quoted this Scripture to me: *"Husbands, love your wives, just as Christ also loved the church AND GAVE HIMSELF FOR HER" (Ephesians 5:25).* I then understood that until Jesus' death, He did not seek to have His wife the church to be a companion or to bring Him comfort. He gave up His own need of companionship. Instead, He poured His life into His bride, the church. The reason Jesus did this is so *"THAT HE MIGHT SANCTIFY AND CLEANSE HER ...THAT HE MIGHT PRESENT HER TO HIMSELF A GLORIOUS CHURCH [WIFE], not having spot or wrinkle or any such thing, but that she should be holy and without blemish. SO HUSBANDS OUGHT TO LOVE THEIR OWN WIVES..." (Ephesians 5:26-28).*

It follows that a husband is to lay aside his main need, choosing to continually meet the primary need of his wife by pouring his life into her. She, in turn, becomes the companion that the husband so desperately needs. The seed to the husband's own need for companionship is found in the very affection he gives to his wife. This affection "seed" goes deep into the womb of his wife's heart, germinates, and companionship is birthed toward her husband. This is the cycle of unity or oneness in a family. The husband lays aside his need for companionship and meets his wife's need for affection. After his wife becomes pregnant with companionship from the seed of affection, she in turn becomes that loving friend the husband so desperately needs. If there is no unity or oneness in a marriage, this cycle is broken. The wife by herself is unable to produce out of herself the companionship for her husband unless there is already a common interest. The source of unity in the family flows out of the wife's heart. However, she alone is unable to bring unity to her family no matter how hard she tries. The husband himself cannot birth unity because he only carries the seed. **HENCE, THE HUSBAND MUST *FIRST* PLANT THE SEED OF AFFECTION IN HIS WIFE'S HEART, *THEN* UNITY WILL FLOW OUT AND THEY WILL BECOME ONE.**

When the husband is pouring affection into his wife's heart, she in turn becomes his companion and friend. As this is combined with an intimate sexual relationship, the marriage will be one of the most fulfilling and satisfying experiences of life. The husband and wife must never withhold proper sex from each other for wrong motives, such as unforgiveness or "teaching them a lesson." *"Let the husband RENDER to his wife THE AFFECTION DUE her [Notice this happens first!], and likewise, also the wife to her husband. The wife does not have authority over her own body, but the husband does. And likewise, the husband does not have authority over his own body, but the wife does. DO NOT DEPRIVE ONE ANOTHER EXCEPT WITH CONSENT [BOTH HUSBAND AND WIFE AGREEING] FOR A TIME, that you may give yourselves to fasting and prayer; AND COME TOGETHER AGAIN so that satan does not tempt you because of your lack of self-control"* (1Corinthians 7:3-5).

A COMPLETE MARRIAGE

A marriage relationship is built over a lifetime. There are four kinds of "love" needed to make a marriage relationship complete. They are *AGAPE, PHILEO, STORGE,* and *EROS.* All are essential in a marriage.

The highest form of these types of love is *agape. Agape* love is an unselfish committed love. It loves when all other types of love quit, and cares when there is no apparent reason to care. This love comes from God into a person when they ask Jesus to come into their heart and to be their Lord and Savior. God is our example. He *"...demonstrates HIS OWN LOVE [agape] toward us, in that while we were STILL SINNERS, CHRIST DIED FOR US"* (Romans 5:8). He likewise commands all husbands to *"...love [agape] your wives AS CHRIST ALSO LOVED THE CHURCH AND GAVE HIMSELF FOR HER"* (Ephesians 5:25).

People make friends with others according to the kind of car they drive or what kind of clothes they wear, or their status in society. The *agape* love of God goes past the surface, enabling us to look deep into our mate's heart and love them for who God has made them to be despite their faults and shortcomings. *Agape* is a committed love, not an unconditional love.

Phileo love is the kind of love that makes *agape* love enjoyable. *Phileo* love is having tender affection toward your mate. Most friendships are built on *phileo* love. *Phileo* love is that "something" that you see in another person that draws you to be their friend. It's one thing to unselfishly commit yourself to love (*agape*) someone who you don't like to be around because they irritate you. It's quite another thing to unselfishly commit yourself to love someone who is tenderly affectionate (*phileo*) toward you. **THE TENDER AFFECTION OF *PHILEO* LOVE MAKES THE UNSELFISH COMMITTED LOVE OF *AGAPE* ENJOYABLE.** It's the joy of the friendship!

It has been said that *phileo* love is a human love. If that were the case, then why does God the Father, who is NOT a human, but a Spirit, *phileo* love Jesus His Son and us? Jesus said, *"For the FATHER HIMSELF LOVES (phileo) YOU, because you have loved (phileo) Me..."* (John 16:27).

God's desire for the husband and wife is that they tenderly love (*phileo*) each other while they overlook each other's faults and failures (*agape*).

Another kind of love needed in a marriage is *storge*. *Storge* is a physical show of affection that results from a pure motive. It may be a hug, a kiss, or another expression of genuine affection. Because males are different than females, the wife usually needs this kind of love more from her husband. It is important for the husband to set aside his need of companionship and meet his wife's main need, which is affection.

Eros love is needed to make a marriage. *Eros* is the fulfillment of the physical sexual desire that a husband and wife show toward each other. It's when *"...the two ...become ONE FLESH" (Matthew 19:5)*.

When all four types of love operate in a marriage, the marriage is complete. A picture of a complete marriage is a husband and wife who lay down their life for each other (*agape* love) no matter how many times the other offends them or causes them to have ill feelings. They both have tender affection toward each other (*phileo* love). They enjoy each other's company because they're best friends. Because they enjoy each other so much, they hug, kiss, hold hands and do nice things for their mate (*storge* love). Because their hearts are filled with *agape, phileo* and *storge*, a warm passionate desire arises within both of them to enjoy each other sexually (*eros*). Now, that kind of God-centered marriage will weather ANY storm.

We must nurture and protect ALL of these different kinds of love in our marriage. Negligence of any kind of love leaves a gaping hole in our relationship. To show you the significance and impact of this on our relationship, let's remove one type of love at a time and see how incomplete the other three are alone.

THE MISSING LINK

Let's take out the highest form of love first, *agape*. Since *agape* love is unselfish the thing that will be prevalent, is selfishness. Human nature in itself is very selfish. *Agape* love influences and dominates all the other types of love. Selfishness will dominate *phileo* love. The friendship of the relationship will have a predominate undertone of "how can the friendship satisfy ME." "If I act a certain pleasing way, I can get this." *Storge*, that physical show of affection will diminish because "self" does not see it as important unless IT wants something. *Eros*, the passionate desire for sex, becomes one sided.

When *phileo* love is missing, the selfless committed love of *agape* will still be intact, but there will be a lack of friendship in the marriage. That gooey show of affection of *storge* will not be as prevalent. The need for sex of *eros* love will be more out of honor or duty.

Storge, that physical show of affection, is normal when *phileo* and *agape* love are intact. *Storge* love is usually missing because of emotional/psychological problems. The wounds that were inflected from trauma, neglect or some other issue of the past must be worked through; otherwise, one partner may feel a measure of rejection because they believe that their partner does not want to be affectionate to them. It's not that they don't want to, but that their heart will not give them the liberty to express it. This, of course will affect the *eros* love. The couple's sex life will diminish. Most likely sex will be a result of need, rather than the passionate desire that arises from the affection of *storge* love.

Notice that the greatest love, *agape*, has the greatest impact. As we descend down the love priority list the impact on the relationship is less, though there will still be significant degradation. All of the different kinds of love are important, but there is a hierarchy of impact.

When all the other types of love are intact, a relationship without *eros* love can survive and do fairly well. The primary reason why there would not be a sexual relationship is because of a physical problem. All the other types of love together would substitute for the feelings and passion of sex but can't replace sex itself.

You can see that a couple is "whole" when: they have worked through the issues of the past, when they work on the essentials of their relationship, when they have a vital relationship with God, then their marriage can be a continual celebration of their friendship. That is what it is supposed to be. There will be challenges, difficulties and disappointments, but that is why we want a strong marriage — to overcome!

7

SUBMISSION

SUBMISSION

There is much confusion concerning submission. We want to be accountable and to submit to others, but we don't know where to draw the line. Often, we don't draw any lines at all, or the lines that we do draw are way past the safety zone. We realize it when we are over our heads in trouble. So where are the lines to be drawn that will keep us safe, walking in truth, and in the center of God's will?

As we explore these safety lines, we must know that whatever we do, whatever we teach, however we pray, we can never do it properly without involving the heart of God. We must have His heart on the matter to know HIS true intentions since He is the Originator of all good things.

As we go over various Scriptures concerning submission, note carefully four very important items. Without knowing these boundary lines, we could be submitting to someone who God doesn't want to control us, perhaps our own spouse.

•Notice first that the submitting we do is to be ONLY to that which is from the heart of God.

•Secondly, there is ALWAYS a resisting to that which is of the devil's heart.

•Thirdly, there is ALWAYS a drawing near to God.

•And fourthly, there is ALWAYS a moving away from that which is evil.

Let's examine these items more closely.

GOD'S RULE GOVERNING SUBMISSION

There is a key to understanding proper submission — submission that is truly ordained of God. This key is found in the Scripture that speaks of the highest order of submission.

THIS IS THE KEY: ALL THAT WHICH THE HIGHEST-ORDER SCRIPTURE SAYS CONCERNING SUBMISSION UNTO GOD, MUST HOLD TRUE FOR ALL SUBORDINATE TYPES OF SUBMISSION SCRIPTURES AS WELL. There are servant Scriptures, and there are master Scriptures. *"A servant is not greater than his master" (John 15:20a)*. The following Scripture is a master, the highest-order Scripture regarding submission. ALL other (servant) Scriptures concerning submission cannot carry their own meaning apart from their master. The servant or subordinate Scriptures carry the heart of the master Scripture.

Let's take a look at the highest-order Scripture for submission:

"Therefore SUBMIT TO GOD [and not to the devil], [but] RESIST THE DEVIL ...[and] DRAW NEAR TO GOD..." (James 4:7,8).

This is the highest order of submission that we "submit to God." God Himself is the Highest! Notice that in submitting to God we are to "resist the devil." If we are to submit to God, we are submitting to His thoughts and His ways. If we are to resist the devil, we are to resist his thoughts and his ways.

The Bible says to *"Let the wicked FORSAKE HIS WAY, and the unrighteous man his THOUGHTS; Let him RETURN [TO THE WAYS AND THOUGHTS OF] THE LORD..." (Isaiah 55:7)*. The Lord is saying that those who have submitted to and embraced any other "thoughts" and any other "ways" than His, have sinned and gone AWAY from the Lord. That's why He says to "return." The Lord continues, *"For My thoughts are not your thoughts, nor are your ways My ways..." (Isaiah 55:8)*. Why did the Lord say that His thoughts and His ways were not ours, and our ways not His? Because we have accepted someone else's thoughts and ways and rejected His. **SUBMISSION AND REBELLION ARE ALWAYS FOR OR AGAINST SOMEONE'S**

THOUGHTS OR WAYS. God wants us to return and submit ONLY to His thoughts and His ways. His thoughts and His ways are only known by knowing Him personally and by knowing what is written in His Word, the Bible.

If we return to His ways of thinking and acting, the Scriptures promise: that we *"...shall go out with joy, and be led with peace; the mountains and hills shall break forth into singing before you ...INSTEAD OF THE THORN shall come up the cypress tree, and INSTEAD OF THE BRIER shall come up the myrtle tree..." (Isaiah 55:12,13)*. Therefore, if we submit ourselves to someone that leads us to violate God's Word or our conscience, we are submitting to the devil instead of resisting him. In reality, we resist God.

This highest-order submission Scripture says to "draw near to God." As we submit to anyone, we should be drawing near to God. Of course, our own selfishness can keep us from drawing closer to God while we submit to another. It may appear like we're submitting, but we do not have the right attitude or motive in our heart. The right attitude and motive is to please God in all ways. The submission experience should transform us into the likeness of Jesus Christ Himself. If we are submitting to the lies of the devil, we are being drawn to our enemy and becoming like him. We are constantly being changed. That change depends upon who is our lord: God and His instructions, or the devil and his instructions.

SUBMISSION ALWAYS HAS RESISTANCE

Let's examine the subordinate submission Scriptures in light of our submission to God. Godly submission is always "to God" and "against the devil." Satanic submission, or satan worship is always "to satan" and "against God." **SUBMISSION ALWAYS HAS RESISTANCE.** When you're submitting to God by surrendering control to Him, you must resist the "other god." If you are submitting to the devil and his deeds, you are resisting God. Submission ALWAYS includes surrender AND resistance. For *"no man can serve TWO masters..." (Matthew 6:24a)*.

The highest-order submission Scripture tells us to submit yourself to God: *"Therefore, SUBMIT TO GOD [and not to the devil]. [But] RESIST THE DEVIL ...[AND] DRAW NEAR TO GOD..." (James 4:7,8).*

The subordinate submission Scriptures tells wives to submit to their OWN husbands: *"Wives, SUBMIT to your own husbands, AS TO THE LORD" (Ephesians 5:22).*

Notice that wives are not to submit to "another man," but the man of the marriage. More importantly, the submission to the man of the marriage is "AS TO THE LORD." What does "as to the Lord" mean? And to whom is submission rendered? "As to the Lord" is the way a Christian ought to submit to others. Whether it is our spouses, our employer, or those who are in law enforcement or government authorities, the submission that we render to them is the same submission that we would render to the Lord Jesus Himself — "as [we would submit] to the Lord." Meaning, God commands us to resist evil no matter what form it comes in and no matter who it comes through.

We have been taught that we are to blindly follow our spouse, but that is just not true. God set up specific guidelines in His written Word for us so we will not be deceived and do wrong. Gods' written Word is our foundation. His Holy Spirit will lead and guide us according to that Word. The Lord Himself would not have anyone do anything ungodly (evil) or under coercion or manipulation. In a marriage, submitting "as to the Lord" is submitting to that which is OF THE LORD in your spouse.

For instance, let's say that an angle spoke to us to do something evil, we would have NO choice but to resist and say, "No!" The Word of God, which is our instructions on how to submit, says to *"Abhor what is evil. Cling to what is good. Resist the devil ...[and] draw near to God..." (Romans 12:9, James 4:7,8),* NO MATTER WHO IT IS! Even if it's *"...an angel from heaven ...let him be accursed" (Galatians 1:8).* The Scripture says to *"cling to what is good" (Romans 12:9c).* **CLINGING IS SUBMITTING! WHEN IT'S "OF THE LORD," YOU SUBMIT "AS TO THE LORD." WHEN IT'S *NOT* "OF THE LORD," YOU DON'T SUBMIT "AS TO THE LORD."** For example, you are not to submit to abuse; it's not "of the Lord."

SUBMISSION TO THOSE IN AUTHORITY

Submitting to those of God in ministry: *"...the household of Stephanas ...have DEVOTED THEMSELVES TO THE MINISTRY OF THE SAINTS — that you also SUBMIT TO SUCH, and to everyone who works and labors..." (1Corinthians 16:15,16).*

Those in ministry, to whom we are to submit, must be "devoted" to loving God and His people. They must abhor and resist evil themselves. We must resist any evil that comes from them. That is true love for God! How can we love God without hating and resisting evil?

Submitting to those in civil authority: *"Obey those who rule over you, and BE SUBMISSIVE, for THEY WATCH OUT FOR YOUR SOULS, AS THOSE WHO MUST GIVE ACCOUNT" (Hebrews 13:17).*

"Therefore SUBMIT YOURSELVES to every ordinance [law] of man FOR THE LORD'S SAKE, whether to the king as supreme, or to governors, as to those who are sent by him FOR THE PUNISHMENT OF EVILDOERS AND FOR THE PRAISE OF THOSE WHO DO GOOD. For this is the will of God..." (1Peter 2:13-15).

The command to the one in authority is to "watch out for your soul." They are to look out for our welfare. They are there "for the punishment of evildoers and for the praise of those who do good." Do you see the resistance to evil and the clinging to that which is good in these authorities to whom we are to submit? When governing authorities make laws outside the will of God (such as the convenience of killing innocent children by means of aborting), and go beyond His Law (the Bible), we no longer are commanded by God to submit to those man-made laws. We are to resist them and have them changed.

SUBMISSION TO ONE ANOTHER

Submitting to one another: *"...Be FILLED WITH THE SPIRIT ...SUBMITTING to one another IN THE FEAR OF GOD"* (Ephesians 5:18,21).

The Scripture says to "be filled with (or controlled by) the [Holy] Spirit." Would God tell us to "resist the devil" if He Himself does not resist him? Of course not! When we are filled with His Holy Spirit, His Spirit in us resists that which is evil. That's why God wants us to be filled with Himself. We need to be able to discern what's of God and what's not.

To sum up these Scriptures concerning submission, God is saying two main things:

First, *"be holy, for I am holy" (1 Peter 1:16)*. When one submits to God, they submit to holiness. God may be manifested through a person, place or thing.

And second, we are not to *"...give place to the devil" (Ephesians 4:27)*. When we resist the devil, he has no "place" in our life. In whatever form he manifests himself, we are to resist, giving him NO place. If we submit to him in any form, we sin and take on his likeness, until we repent. **WE BECOME THAT WHICH WE SUBMIT TO OR EMBRACE.** It may be our husbands or wives, our government officials or employer, those who are in the ministry of God or one another. They must fulfill their godly role to stand against evil. If they choose evil, they bring evil upon those for whom they are responsible and we are no longer under command to submit. Evil is anything unrighteous, morally wrong or bad, wicked, or anything that is outside of God's will that He has revealed to us.

Because we live in dangerous times, God gave us guidelines to use as we submit to one another. *"See then that you walk circumspectly, [meaning, careful to consider all related circumstances before acting, judging, deciding, etc.] not as fools but as wise, redeeming the time, because the days are evil. Therefore, DO NOT BE UNWISE, but UNDERSTAND WHAT THE WILL OF THE LORD IS ...be filled with the Spirit ...SUBMITTING to one another IN THE FEAR OF GOD" (Ephesians 5:15-18,21)*. We are to "fear the Lord" and not man. YOU SUBMIT TO WHOMEVER YOU FEAR. God wants us to fear Him only. If we fear anyone or anything else, we will submit to them as our god. That's why many people are afraid to break off a relationship; they fear them and so they serve them. *"...Choose for yourselves this day whom YOU will serve..." (Joshua 24:15).*

SUBMISSION TO SPOUSE

Submission to our spouse is never greater than our submission to God. Some people actually think God gives us the liberty to have another god before us. That is just not so (See Exodus 20:3). We must always submit to God first. He knows what decisions to make. As we submit to God and to one another He uses these situations to mature us, to bless us, and to reveal our own weaknesses. This results in our seeking Him all the more. *"For when I am weak, THEN I am strong" (2Corinthians 12:10b).*

There are all kinds of daily situations where one must submit to another. Husbands and wives need to make decisions daily about certain things. These decisions are not always to separate the good from the evil, but deciding what's the best thing to do in a particular situation.

For example, we may need a car, but what kind? How much do we spend? These kinds of situations are where we grow together as husband and wife while submitting to one another. We must gain understanding of what kind of car fits our needs so we can make a wise decision. At times it is not always clear which course of action to take. This is where praying together in agreement comes in — seeking Gods heart together. Even though a better automobile may be needed, which one is the right one for us?

Suppose the wife felt that "THIS car is the one." But the husband isn't sure which car to get. What could happen next? The husband could override his wife and say no, or the husband could trust the Lord through his wife and submit to her after they talked it out. In these kinds of daily decisions, **IT'S BETTER FOR THE HUSBAND AND WIFE TO BE IN AGREEMENT AND SUBMIT TO EACH OTHER EVEN IF IT'S THE WRONG CHOICE.** The choice could be wrong because of a lack of knowledge. Therefore, it is better to submit to each other instead of being in disagreement, which causes strife. It is God's heart to make right a wrong situation when the couple is in agreement seeking Him even if they did make the wrong choice. It is better to be in agreement and make a wrong choice with a clean conscience than for one spouse to disagree and make the "right" choice and be in constant strife. *"For where envy and self-seeking [strife] exist, CONFUSION AND EVERY EVIL THING ARE THERE" (James 3:16).*

HAVING GOD'S HEART IN SUBMISSION

When we submit to someone, we are actually submitting to the Christ in them or the satan in them. Let me clarify. In each verse of Scripture we just read concerning submitting to another, there are commands to submit only to that which is of God: That which does not violate the Word of God, our conscience, or that which God has dealt with us about in our own personal lives concerning His purpose for us. When we know we haven't violated the Word of God, we have a clean conscience and our heart is open and receptive before Him. We know we have then properly submitted, even if the spouse doesn't agree. We are not to make gods of others in our attitude of submission. God is jealous for that position alone (See Exodus 20:4,5). The church seems to have forgotten that God doesn't want us to have any other gods before us, no matter what form they come in, even if they are our husbands and wives.

Many times we are placed in a position where we must submit to the one God has in authority over us. They may be arrogant or belligerent, but this is where we as Christians are called to grow. These times are to teach us humility, to give us opportunity to expand the character of God in us, and to be a visible witness of Who and what God is like. God uses all these character defects in us to build more patience, to grow fruits of kindness, to destroy pride and to grow in us all those virtues of Jesus. We do not want to escape these kinds of situations. God wants us to walk THROUGH them so WE will be changed while demonstrating righteousness — righteous acts of God. Perhaps then, we may be able to help the one with the speck in their eye (See Matthew 7:3,4).

8

CLOSING WORDS

DOING THE RIGHT THING, TOO LONG

I know we have covered a lot of ground, but let me share some final things with you in closing. God's desire and mine is that every husband and wife enjoys each other to the fullest. Marriages are very special before the Lord, but the people in the marriages are even more special.

There are many couples who are enjoying their marriage. There are also couples who find their marriage like an anchor around their neck pulling them under water for the third time. A proper marriage is very wonderful and very beautiful; however, it is possible to stay in a wrong or bad marriage and be doing the "right thing" too long. The story of God testing Abraham to sacrifice his only son Isaac is a good example of this:

The Lord told Abraham to *"...Take ...your only son Isaac, whom you love and go ...and offer him there as a burnt offering..."* (Genesis 22:2). So Abraham listened to God and tied up Isaac and placed him upon an alter that he made. *"And Abraham stretched out his hand and took the knife to slay his son. But the Angel of the Lord called to him from heaven and said, 'Abraham, Abraham ...DO NOT LAY YOUR HAND ON THE LAD, OR DO ANYTHING TO HIM; for now I know that you fear God, since you have not withheld your son, your only son, from me'"* (Genesis 22:10-12).

What if Abraham missed the Lord's voice telling him to STOP THE SACRIFICE? What if Abraham had kept doing the last thing he was supposed to do? Isaac would have been dead! If we miss the Word of God or the voice of God and continue in a bad or wrong marriage longer than we're supposed to, we, too, can become a sacrifice that was not intended. God does not want us to be a "sacrificial victim" for the "sake of the marriage." Just as God told Abraham to stop the sacrifice of his son, so God speaks to us who are in dead marriages to stop being a sacrificial victim for the sake of the marriage institution. Jesus Himself said to those who esteemed the institution to be greater than those who make up the institution, *"...IF ONLY YOU HAD KNOWN WHAT THIS SAYING MEANS, I desire [to have] mercy ...RATHER THAN ...[to have] sacrificial victims, YOU WOULD NOT HAVE CONDEMNED THE GUILTLESS"* (Matthew 12:7 AMP).

Many good books have been written that deal with how to promote and build strong marriages. Thank God for them; we need them. However, there are very few books that deal with the "need to divorce." We must not view the divorce of a bad marriage as an end of something good, because it is not. If the marriage were good, there wouldn't be any divorce. It's the end of something that went bad, and the BEGINNING of something new.

God loves you more than you know. He sacrificed and raised from the dead His only Son so we wouldn't go to hell and that we will be able to live life to the fullest.

If you have never asked the Lord Jesus to come into your heart, I extend His invitation to you. He paid a debt for your sin that only He could satisfy. He is your only hope. He will be the strength and comfort you so desperately need during this time. Open your heart and receive Him. Don't be afraid. God wants to love you more than you want to be loved. Say this confession now and let God's love flow into your heart and give peace to your mind. These words will not be worth anything unless they are YOUR words. Meaning, they MUST originate from YOUR heart as YOUR words. Say something like this out loud to God:

Dear Lord Jesus, I need help. I need a savior, and I'm asking you to come into my heart and to fill me with your divine love. Jesus, I confess you as my Lord and the payment for my sins. Take my life and turn it into something wonderful. Lord, I ask you to fill me with your Holy Spirit, power, ability and wisdom, so that I can successfully live for you. Thank you Lord for loving me. Amen.

Now that you have called upon the Lord to save you, YOU must make a simple confession out loud to SOMEONE. When you read the question, read it out-loud so that you could hear it with your own ears and then answer the question out-loud with a simple "yes" or "no." It is very important. The question is: Do you believe that Jesus the Lord died for your sins and that God raised Jesus from the dead?

Be sure to tell someone that you believe Jesus died for your sins and that God raised Him from the dead. It is vital!

After speaking this and believing this from your heart, you will feel God's peace come into your heart, and feel like a burden has rolled off your shoulders. You are now born again.

This book is not intended for everyone. Not everyone is stuck in an abusive marriage. Not every marriage is out of God's will.

What God has given me, I have shared with you: the answers to these complex and misunderstood questions concerning marriage, divorce, remarriage, interracial marriage and submission. Because they are the TRUTH, does not change the fact that divorce hurts and can be a difficult road. But know this, the God of all creation, the One who loves you enough to send you these Words of Truth, is the One who will walk you through this difficult time. Just ask Him. He will never leave you nor forsake you — ever. Trust Him above all else. He is your strength in time of trouble.

The Introduction Scripture may now have more meaning: *"...Those who are well have no need of a physician, BUT THOSE WHO ARE SICK. But go and learn what this means: 'I DESIRE [FOR YOU] MERCY AND NOT [FOR YOU TO BE A] SACRIFICE'"* (Matthew 9:12,13).

If you need help, don't forget to look through the SOURCES section in the rear of this book. Or, you may visit our website listed below to view our updated list.

To order another book for a friend or to drop us a line, visit us on the web or write:

DivorceHope
PO Box 640
301 N. Main St.
Coudersport, PA 16915 USA

Email: info@divorcehope.com
Web Address: http://www.DivorceHope.com
Internet Christian Book Store Web Address:
http://ChristianBookStores.SpreadTheWord.com

NOTES

1. (Page 38,41) <u>Amplified Bible, Expanded Edition</u>, (1987), Published by Zondervan Corporation and the Lockman Foundation, Page 543, last sentence of note.

2. (Page 42) <u>Answers Update</u>, Published by Answers In Genesis Ministries, PO Box 6330, Florence, KY 41022, Volume 9, Issue II, Page 16(back page).

3. (Page 47) <u>The Nations</u>, by C.B. Peter Morgan, (1992), published by Destiny Image, P.O. Box 310, Shippensburg, PA 17257, Page 7.

4. (Page 48) Ibid, Page 7.

5. (Page 48) Ibid, Page 6,7.

6. (Page 54) <u>Hill Country Wanderings</u> (May 1998), RR1 Box 297, Austin, PA 16720, Volume 2, Issue 2, Page 5.

7. (Page 70) <u>The New Strong's Exhaustive Concordance of the Bible</u>, (1984), Published by Thomas Nelson, Inc., Nashville, Tennessee, Greek Word #1515.

8. (Page 91) Ibid, Greek word #5563.

9. (Page 92) Ibid, Greek word #22.

10. (Page 92) Ibid, Greek word #1062.

11. (Page 110) Ibid, Greek word #630.

12. (Page 117) <u>Webster's American Family Dictionary</u> (1998), Published by Random House, Inc., 201 East 50th St, New York, NY 10022, page 1068.

13. (Page 117) Ibid, Page 413.

14. (Page 117) Ibid, Page 277.

15. (Page 117) Ibid, Page 1068.

16. (Page 117) <u>The New Strong's Exhaustive Concordance of the Bible</u>, (1984), Published by Thomas Nelson, Inc., Nashville, Tennessee Greek words #488, 490, 491.

    "Widow" and "widowhood" are from the same Hebrew word that means: "Discarded (as a divorced person), forsaken.

    Alman, (Strong's #488) = Discarded (as a divorced person), forsaken.

    Almanah, (Strong's #490) = A widow. [Almanah is the feminine of Alman].

    Almanuwth, (Strong's #491) = Widowhood. [Almanuwth is the feminine of Alman].

17. (Page 121) Ibid, Hebrew word #7676 (from #7673).

18. (Page 86) Ibid, Hebrew word #7971.

APPENDIX

MY TRANSLATION

All numbers in brackets "(#)" are from the Greek dictionary of The New Strong's Exhaustive Concordance of the Bible.

1 Corinthians 7:27-28a

Are you bound [married] to a wife? Do not seek to be DIVORCED (#3089). Are you DIVORCED (#3080) from a wife? Do not seek a wife. But EVEN IF YOU DO MARRY, YOU HAVE NOT SINNED...

Matthew 1:19

Then Joseph her [engaged] husband, being a JUST MAN, and not wanting to make her a public example, was minded to RELEASE HER BY BREAKING OFF (#630) [the engagement] secretly.

Matthew 19:3-9

The Pharisees also came to Him, testing Him, and saying to Him, "Is it lawful for a man to release and separate (#630) [from] his wife [without divorcing her] for just any reason?" And He answered and said to them, "Have you not read that He who made them at the beginning 'made them male and female'" and said, "for this reason a man shall leave his father and mother and be joined to his wife, and the two shall become one flesh? So then they are no longer two but one flesh."

Jesus is saying, "haven't you read that if a married couple separates without an actual divorce, they are still 'joined' as 'one flesh'. And if they remarry in that condition they are in adultery." In the beginning the Lord never wanted the husband and wife to separate without a divorce. Otherwise, they could not become another man's wife or another woman's husband (See Deuteronomy 24:1,2).

"Therefore what God has joined together, let not man separate." They said to Him, "Why then did Moses COMMAND to give a certificate of divorce (#647), AND to release and separate from (#630) her?"

These Pharisees still don't seem to understand why they have to give a certificate of divorce when they separate from their wives!

He said to them, "Moses, BECAUSE OF THE HARDNESS OF YOUR HEARTS, PERMITTED you to release and separate (#630) from your wives [without a certificate of divorce (#647)]. But from the beginning [being released and separated (#630) WITHOUT a certificate of divorce (#647)] was not so. And I say to you, whoever releases and separates (#630) from his wife [without a certificate of divorce (#647)], except for sexual immorality, and marries another, commits adultery; and whoever marries her who is separated (#630) [without being divorced] commits adultery."

150

SOURCES

This list was accurate as this book went to press. This list is only a sample from all the great sources of help. Even though the author is not affiliated with, nor endorsed by any person, company, or ministry listed in this section, we have been associated with or had experience with many of them through the years.

BOOKS ON "BREAKING CURSES"

Marilyn Hickey Ministries
(Prayer line, book and tape resources.)
1-877-661-1249 (M-F 6:30am-4:30pm, MST, USA only).
Web Address: **www.mhmin.org**

Book: "BREAKING GENERATIONAL CURSES"
          Published by: Harrison House

Eagles Nest Ministries
(Book and tape resources.)
1-714-429-7888
Web Address: **www.eaglesnestministries.org/home**

Book: "SEDUCTIONS EXPOSED"
          Published by: Whitaker House.

PRAYER LINES, BOOKS AND TAPES

Joyce Meyers Ministries
(Books and tapes for healing from abuse and difficult upbringing, prayer, listen to broadcast.)
1-800-707-7877
Prayer Line: 1-866-349-3300 (M-F 6am-6pm CST).
Web Address: **www.joycemeyer.org**
(On home page, select button, "HELP FOR THE HURTING.")

FamilyLife
(Books, tapes, listen online.)
1-800-358-6329
Web Address: **www.familylife.com**

Kenneth Copeland Ministries
(Books, tapes, listen/view online, church online, prayer.)
Web Address: **www.kcm.org**

Time For Hope
(Mental Health, referrals, all kinds of resources.)
Television host: Dr. Freda V. Crews
1-800-669-9133
Web Address: **www.timeforhope.org**

COUNSELING/THERAPY/PRAYER/HELP

Dawson McAllister Association
(HOPE-line 1-800-394-HOPE [4673], open Sun-Sat 6pm-1PM CST.)
Chaplain and live help desk, listen online, other resources.
Prayer Web Address: **www.theprayerroom.com**

New Life Ministries
(Books, tapes, counselor/therapist referrals only, listen online.)
1-800-NEW LIFE (639-5433)
Web Address: **www.newlife.com**

Meier Clinic
(Therapist/counselors, books and tapes.)
1-888-7CLINIC (725-4642), 24hours a day help line.
Web Address: **www.meierclinics.com**
(NOTICE, "meierclinic.com" is **NOT** their web site; "clinics" has an "s.")

American Association of Christian Counselors (AACC)
(Locate a counselor, books.)
1-434-525-9470
Web Address: **www.aacc.net**

American Counseling Association
(National Counseling Referral Directory)
(Referral network of behavioral health care professionals for in-office, telephone and email counseling and therapist.)
1-866-721-1101
Web Address: **www.personalsolutions.com**
Web Address: **www.counseling.org**

Focus on the Family
(Books, tapes and counseling line.)
1-800-A-FAMILY (232-6459) (For resources, or ask for correspondence or counseling to talk with someone).
Counseling Dept. direct line, 1-719-531-3400
Web Address: **www.family.org**

Forensic Financial Divorce Analysis
(Divorce Planning Consultant: Analyzing your financial situation in case of or for a divorce. Free initial consultation for anyone by J.P. Morgan, D.Min., CDFA,CDS.)
1-904-261-5483
Web Address: **www.themagdoc.com**

Smalley Relationship Center
(Counseling, books and tapes.)
1-866-875-2915 (Other crisis emergency numbers given when calling this number. Available M-F 8am-5pm CST).
Web Address: **www.smalleyonline.com**

ABUSE/ADDICTION/DISORDER REFERRALS/RESOURCES

National Association For Research And Therapy Of Homosexuality
(Specialty: Homosexuality help, resources.)
1-818-789-4440
Web Address: **www.narth.com**

Faithful And True Ministries
(Specialty: Sexual addiction.)
Web address: **www.faithfulandtrueministries.com**

Sex Addict
(Specialty: Sexual addiction recovery resources, telephone counseling.)
1-719-278-3708
Web address: **www.sexaddict.com**

National Association For Christian Recovery
(Abuse/addiction/disorder referrals.)
1-714-529-6227
Web Address: **nacronline.com** ("Referral Center" button).
Web Address: **www.spiritualabuse.com**

Cloud-Townsend Resources
(Solutions For Life, resources, referrals.)
1-800-676-HOPE (4673)
Web Address: **www.cloudtownsend.com** (Excellent tape library. "Tape Library" button).

Marriage Builders
(Specializing in saving marriages from divorce. Using the best ways to overcome marital conflicts and to restore love. Phone marriage & divorce counseling.)
1-651-762-8570
Web Address: **www.marriagebuilders.com**

Troubled With
(Immediate help. Free counseling help available for ANY kind of problem or situation.)
1-866-914-HOPE (4673) for resources,
1-719-531-3400 for free counseling.
Web Address: **www.troubledwith.com**